Elfi H. M. Gilissen
German Slang — the real German
published by
REISE KNOW-HOW Verlag Peter Rump GmbH
Osnabrücker Str. 79, D-33649 Bielefeld
info@reise-know-how.de

© REISE KNOW-HOW Verlag Peter Rump GmbH
4th edition 2015

Revision	Elfi H.M. Gilissen
Layout	Elfi H.M. Gilissen
Layout Conception	Günter Pawlak, FaktorZwo! Bielefeld
Cover	Peter Rump, Coverfoto: © Kristine Jaath
Illustrations	©Andrew Tokmakoff (p. 1, 24, 28, 33, 53, 58, 63, 89, 94, 98, 105, 109, 118, 128, 130, 132, 136),
	©Rosa Gilissen (p. 43, 46, 64, 72, 78, 123, 140)
	©Yuri Arcurs@Fotolia.com (p. 39)
Print & Binding	Werbedruck GmbH Horst Schreckhase, Spangenberg

ISBN 978-3-8317-6465-5
Printed in Germany

This book is available in every bookshop in Germany, Austria,
Switzerland and Benelux. If you can't find it, please ask your
bookseller to order it from one of the distributors listed below:

Germany	Prolit GmbH, Postfach 9, 35461 Fernwald (Annerod)
Switzerland	AVA-buch 2000, Postfach 27, CH-8910 Affoltern
Austria	Mohr Morawa Buchvertrieb GmbH,
	Sulzengasse 2, A-1230 Wien
Belgium & Netherlands	Willems Adventure, www.willemsadventure.nl
directly	http://www.reise-know-how.de

This book is accompanied by audio material
containing all words and phrases in this book,
spoken by a German native speaker.

Are you interested in becoming a Kauderwelsch author?
Take a look at
www.reise-know-how.de/rkh_mitarbeit.php

Kauderwelsch

Elfi H. M. Gilissen

German Slang

– the real German

REISE KNOW-HOW
im Internet
www.reise-know-how.de
info@reise-know-how.de

For smartphone users
(use any scan QR code reader)

audio samples & more information!

Audio samples are also available
on our website:
www.reise-know-how.de/kauderwelsch/188

This slang guide is different!

Why? You are familiar with a foreign language – but when it comes to casual talking you won't understand much. Especially when exploring the "scene", sharing their day-to-day life with ordinary people, chatting with somebody in the street or having a beer together in the pub, you'll discover their language is miles away from what you were taught at school.

What you hear is **colloquial speech**, complemented by somewhat trendy **slang expressions,** often not even familiar to the whole population, but only to certain age groups, members of a scene or fringe groups.

Most slang expressions have a poor life expectancy and won't ever make their way into an official dictionary. **Slang is volatile.** But it makes a dry "standard language" conversation more spicy.

The genuine diversity of a language consists of this lively composition of standard language, colloquial language and slang.

This colourful mixture reflects the way of life, the attitude and the philosophy of the people using it.

Since casual language is rather spoken than written, there are hardly any rules on how to spell these words, so that you might find different spellings of the same word, if you find it written at all.

The authors will make you smile every now and again, making you familiar with the mentality and way of life in the particular language area.

Words, phrases and expressions, used every day, in the pub, at work, in the "scene" and in the street, will be explained. The annex provides you with about 1000 key words to look up in the book when you hear them somewhere – words you'll probably never find in a dictionary.

Contents

Contents

9 Preface
11 How To Use This Book
12 Say It In German
16 Very Peculiar: Denglisch!
20 German Dialects

Colloquialisms & Idioms

26 Yes. Maybe. Sure.
    – a collection of affirmatives
31 No! No Need! As If!
    – all the replies meaning 'no'
35 Great! Not Bad! Wow!
    – when you just love it
40 Shit! No Good!
    – if it's a bunch of crap
47 Kiss My Arse! Who Cares!
    – whenever you could't care less
50 Really? Full On! Stunning!
    – for amazing moments in life
55 Feel Great! Excited! Lucky Me!
    – when you're spirits fly high
59 Exhausted! Wrong! Screwed Up!
    – if everything turns into chaos
65 Hilarious! Joke! Fooled!
    – for all more and less amusing encounters
69 Nonsense! Huh? No Clue!
    – when puzzled about all that bullshit

Contents

73 Chat, Gossip & Whinge
 – *when you can't keep still*

80 Shut Up! Bigmouth! Spit It Out!
 – *if you want the talk or the silence to stop*

83 Crazy! Driving Me Nuts!
 – *whenever someone drives you really mad*

87 Furious! Enough!
 – *when it's all a bit too much*

95 Get Lost! Or Else ...
 – *a collection of last warnings*

100 Pissing Your Pants?
 – *about the scared and the cowardly*

102 Arseholes, Bitches, Idiots & Others
 – *all the fancy curses for both sexes*

112 Cash & Work
 – *the hard-earned crust*

120 Partytime! Get Plastered!
 – *for a good night out*

131 Munch, Devour & Eat
 – *about having something solid to eat*

133 Chatting Up & Knocked Back
 – *for the lovey-doveys*

135 Friends & Sweethearts
 – *for good friends and lovers*

138 About the Body & Intimacy
 – *let's talk about sex*

Annex

144 Sources & Further Reading
145 Index
160 The Author

German Dialects

Preface

Germans have no humour, are always overly formal and uncomfortably blunt. These comments are just as stereotypical as the statement that Germans continuously eat sauerkraut, earning them the post-war nickname 'Krauts'.

Of course there's a grain of truth in these observations. Germans do eat sauerkraut in certain regions and seasons. And yes, they don't have the dry British sense of humour, nor do they generally go for the American slapstick approach, but they certainly do have heaps of humour. It's just exclusively expressed in the German language and if you're not a great connoisseur of their language, you'll undoubtedly miss out on subtleties like humour.

The majority of Germans have rather poor English skills compared to their neighbours, especially Holland and Scandinavia. Even though they (almost) all learnt it at school, their great love for precision which results in their famous high quality cars and zillions of other pieces of craftsmanship 'made in Germany', does inhibit them when asked to use foreign language and communication skills. In the workplace and in social life, they tend to come up with many excuses, why their English is no good and they prefer to speak German.

Thank You!
... to Stephanie-Suzanne Durante *from London* and Dr. George Saunders *from Sydney for their great efforts helping to find the best English equivalents for all the German idioms in this book.*
Also thanks to my partner Andrew Tokmakoff *as well as the above for doing such an excellent job proof-reading it all.*

Preface

The Queen's English surely feels as uptight and serious as its standardised German counterpart **Hochdeutsch.** Whereas the use of local languages and dialects is nowadays no longer suppressed on British TV or radio, **Hochdeutsch** mostly remains a must in the German media. Regional dialects don't have a big place in media presence.

Apart from dialects you also have rules about class and the politically correct way of speaking. However, the man in the street does not always express himself in such a polished way, and even less so when at home, down at the pub or among friends. It's therefore hardly surprising that one can't grasp the jokes being cracked without some serious study of straightforward familiar and outright rude German language. The key to being able to read between the lines is to familiarise yourself with the colloquial expressions and idioms in German.

This little language guide introduces many naughty and funny expressions Germans use in their day-to-day lives when having a casual chat amongst colleagues at work, communicating with family and friends, roaming pubs, bars and clubs, flirting and engaging in sexual relations and when angry or annoyed. The guide can also be of help when you watch a German crime series on TV which is full of rude language. Have fun getting to know the Germans better this way! Yours, Elfi H. M. Gilissen

Also thanks to Christian, Caro, Tom, Michael, Kerstin, Arne, Bart, Anja D. and Anja O. for helping out with little bits and pieces, whenever the web and all available books didn't help to explain an expression and for their ideas on their local dialect.

Last but not least thank you to my mom Rosa Gilissen and my partner Andrew Tokmakoff for the photos illustrating this book, as well as the friends and family depicted on the photographs.

How To Use This Book

The book is mainly meant to promote a better understanding of German colloquialisms and idioms. Even though this eventually can also be helpful to express yourself in German in a less formal manner, I advise you to be very cautious when making use of the rude vocabulary introduced in this book. In regard to the swearwords, bear in mind that until you fully know which expression is appropriate in what type of situation, you are better off not using them yourself – unless you are really looking for a fight. Insults are rarely taken as a mere joke! Even though the English equivalents give you a good idea about the degree of rudeness, we have annotated the rudest ones with a small number one ([1]).

In italics and square brackets *[literal!]* you'll find literal translations of German expressions and idioms, which can be useful to comprehend their original meaning and have some fun analyzing the play on words.

In the following chapters you'll find some simple guidelines to the standard pronunciation of German and a brief guide to the distribution of local dialects in Germany.

In the annex at the end of the book, I have listed sources and further recommended reading, if you'd like to dive further into the world of German idioms and/or dialects.

Kauderwelsch Audio material
If you'd like to hear and practise the pronunciation of the German words and phrases introduced in this book, you can purchase the accompanying audio material in any bookshop in Germany, Austria, Switzerland, the Netherlands and Belgium, online-bookstore or on our internet site (mp-3 download) **www.reise-know-how.de.**

Say It In German

„**D**eutsche Sprache, schwere Sprache", meaning 'German language, difficult language' is what Germans use to say, when someone is struggling with their native tongue. This may be true about the grammar, but when it comes to pronunciation it's far more predictable than English. Just take a moment to familiarise yourself with these basic rules and the first step towards perfect German pronunciation is made! The essentials are:

Short vowels

All German vowels have both a long and a short version. The short version is used when a single vowel is followed by any combination of two (or more) consonants, for example: bb, ch, ck, ll, mm, tz, sch, pf ...

Macker *bloke/boyfriend*	a	like 'u' in 'h**u**m'
lecken *to lick*	e	1) like 'e' in 'w**e**t';
beschissen *shitty*		2) or like 'e' in 'comm**e**nt' when it's the second letter in the prefixes 'ge-, be-, ver-' and in words ending with '-e' or '-e-' plus one consonant, such as '-el, -em, -en, -er, -es, -et ...'
ficken *to fuck*	i	like 'i' in 'b**i**g'
Kotze *puke*	o	like 'o' in 'b**o**ther'
Muschi *cunt*	u	like 'u' in 'p**u**ssy'

Long vowels

The long version is pronounced when a single vowel is followed by only one consonant or an 'h' plus another consonant. The following 'h' always remains silent.

If the same vowel is doubled, it's pronounced like a long vowel as well:

a/ah/aa	like 'a' in 'laugh'	**wahnsinnig** *crazy!*
e/eh/ee	similar to 'ai' in 'raise' or 'a' in 'maze', but without the softening 'i'-sound at the end	**abgedreht** *bewildering*
i/ih	like 'ee' in 'beer'	**Asi** *antisocial person*
o/oh/oo	like 'o' in 'lawnmower' without pronouncing the 'w', but instead stretching the 'o' longer	**Kohle** *money/coal*
u/uh	like 'oo' in 'noodle'	**Hupen** *tits*

'Umlaut' aka the double dots

Typically German are those vowels with double dots, which also differentiate short and long pronunciation. The same rules as for short and long vowels apply.

ä	short like 'e' in 'wet'; for long version stretch to 'weeet'	**beschränkt** *limited* **gähn!** *boring!*
ö	short like 'u' in 'surf'; for long version stretch to 'suuurf'	**beömmeln** *to laugh* **grölen** *to holler*
ü	short like 'ue' in 'muesli' (but much stronger); for long version stretch to 'muueesli'	**Müll** *rubbish* **Hühnerkacke** *shit*

13

Two different vowels in a row

A common combination is a vowel followed by a 'u':

Braut *chick/bride*	**au**	similar to 'ou' in 'cl**ou**d', but shorter
Mäuse *money/mice*	**äu/eu**	like 'oi' in 'm**oi**st'

Apart from these combinations you have 'ie' and 'ei', which are often mixed up by native English speakers:

geil *hot/cool/horny*	**ei**	like 'i' in 'bl**i**nd'
angeschmiert *fooled*	**ie**	like 'ee' in 'b**ee**r'

Consonants

The consonants b, r, sh, t, v, w and x can basically be pronounced the same as in English without creating awkwardness, but others are a little bit more tricky:

Weichei *wimp*	**ch**	the famous 'ch' does really not have an equivalent in English; just imitate German speakers
Wichser *wanker/jerk*	**chs**	like 'x' in 'si**x**'; mostly at end of a word
knuddelig *cute*	**g**	1) at the end of a word in Northern Germany same as a 'ch' (see above);
Gesabbel *drool*		2) at any other position in a word usually like 'g' as in '**g**reen'; also at the end of a word in Southern Germany, Austria and Switzerland

j	generally like 'y' in 'you'	**jammern** *to wail*
s	1) like 's' in 'rose' at the start of a word followed by a vowel and in the middle of a word;	**Möse** *cunt*
	2) like 'ss' in 'boss' at the end of a word and when used as double 's'	**krass** *crass*
ß	since this is considered to be the equivalent for a double-s, it's pronounced like 'ss' in 'boss'	**Scheiße** *shit*
sch	like 'sh' in 'shop'	**bescheuert** *stupid*
sp/st	1) at the end or in the middle of a word like in 'sports' or in 'station';	**knuspern** *to crunch*
		astrein *perfect(ly)*
	2) at the start of a word pronounced like 'shp' or 'sht'	**spitze!** *top!*
		Ständer *erection*
tsch	like 'ch' in 'much'	**Quatsch** *blather*
(t)z	like 'ts' in 'lots'	**Dez** *head*

Exceptions

The above is only true for strictly German words. Words borrowed from English, French or some other language are not quite pronounced like in their country of origin, but rather with a typical German accent.

The spelling in this book is mainly Hochdeutsch, *unless it's never pronounced like that and therefore I've omitted the unspoken vowels to increase your chances of a correct pronunciation.*

For example, French: **Champagner, Journalist, Restaurant, Charmeur, Garage;** Italian: **Radicchio, Gnocchi, Ruccola;** Greek: **Tsatsiki, Gyros, Pita;** Turkish: **Döner, Kebap** etc.

However, an exception in itself is 'y', which can in rare cases be a consonant, but mostly appears as vowel:

y	generally like 'ue' in 'muesli'	**Typ** *(odd) bloke*

Very Peculiar: Denglisch!

Denglisch? Well, for those of you who are not familiar with this term, it's the use of English words in German, but with a bit of a 'twang'. Most of these terms have their origin in the world of IT, marketing, economics, lifestyle, drugs, sports, music and music videos. Denglisch is often not appreciated by language purists, who are only too happy to point their finger at those who use these kind of terms. But in the end, they can scream and shout all they want – you can't police the way people use language!

All the Denglisch terms in this book are marked with a (*) for easy recognition.

Nouns

Since das Handy* looks like an obvious English word, Germans amusingly may think, that it's the correct English term for mobile phone!

Another faux-ami is der Body*, which describes a one piece underwear garment for women (similar to a bathing suit) in German!

Most of the English nouns that are used in German only need a German article, are capitalised and have a German accent added to its pronunciation; a new German word is born! Typically, these terms have less connotations when used in German, unlike their English origins. Some examples: **die Connection*** [influential friends, phone line or link between things/people], **das Casting*** [actors, performers; not cast in a mold, throwing], **das Dinner*** [meal in restaurant or at someone's house for special occasion; not an ordinary family meal!], **das Outfit*** [clothing] ...

However, the plural is often formed in accordance with German pluralisation customs. The article for plural is always **die** and the plural ending may vary. Some get '-en', like **die Beautyfarm(en)***, **die Mailbox(en)***. Words ending in '-er' typically do not obtain a plural ending (only their article will change to plural), like **der Bestseller***, **der Blockbuster***, **der Computer***, **der Eye Catcher***, **der Global Player***, **der Insider***, **das Wellness Center***. Others don't have a plural at all (you cannot even apply the plural article): **das Brunch***, **das Catering***, **das Coming Out***, **das Internet***, **das Recycling***, **der Shit*** ... Sometimes the usual English ending on '-s' is applied for plural: **das Brleting***, **der Hype***, **der Job***, **das Meeting***, **der One-Night-Stand***, **der Quickie***, **die Party***, **der Song***, **das Team***, **der Workflow***, **der Yuppie*** ...

Having proper German articles already indicates that they are inflected just like German nouns in accordance with the gender of the noun (definite or indefinite) and possibly one of the four cases needed within the sentence structure.

In the last spelling reform in Germany 1999 (effective since 2005) it was decided that also English nouns, which consist of more than one word can now be either jointed together with a hyphen or simply be spelled as one word just like typical compound words in German:
das Desktoppublishing*
or Desktop-publishing*,
die Midlifecrisis*
or Midlife-crisis*,
das Happyend*
or Happy-end*,
die Sciencefiction*
or Science-fiction* ...

Der Song* war in den Top Tens* / Toptens* der letzten Monate unter den ersten fünf!
For the past few months this song has been amongst the first five of the top ten!
(**den -s:** definite, plural, accusative case)

Die Story* hat schon so'n Bart!
That's ancient history!

Verbs

A bit more reworking is required for popular English verbs used in German since they firstly need to have the German infinitve ending **-en.** For example: **brunchen*** [to eat brunch], **chillen*** [to chill out, relax], **checken*** [to understand], **downloaden*** [to download from the internet], **killen*** [to kill/stop], **pushen*** [to push ideas], **raten*** [to rate (in the Top Ten)], **toppen*** [to top/exceed, be better], **updaten*** [to update data/software, on gossip], **windsurfen*** [to windsurf], **zappen*** [to zap aimlessly through TV-channels] and some with irregular verb endings like **tricksen*** [to trick] or **ordern*** [to order goods].

The German term for 'to send an SMS' is either SMSen* *or to make it pronounceable with an inserted 'i':* simsen*.

More complex Denglisch words even get typical German prefixes: **abchecken*** [to check], **ein-/auschecken*** [to check in/out (flight/hotel)], **an-/abturnen*** [to turn on/off interest], **aufsplitten*** [to split], **auspowern*** [to waste energy on a task/sport], **verlinken*** [to link website] or they are reflexive: **sich outen*** [to out yourself as a lover/hater of something].

'To email' can also be expressed in two ways: mailen* *or* e-mailen*.

Now they have a proper German infinitive ending they are most certainly inflected just like a German word!

Wir haben gestern lecker gebruncht*.
We had a nice brunch yesterday.

Das turnt* mich einfach ab.
That simply turns me off.

Ich hab mir die Datei down<u>ge</u>loaded* / <u>ge</u>downloaded*.

I downloaded the file.

Denglisch verbs can be used as nouns as well and are then capitalised as per usual in German:

Das Einchecken* am Flughafen nervt!

The check-in at the airport is nerve-racking!

Adjectives

The most prominent example for a Denglisch adjective in idiomatic German is **cool***, which means 'hip', 'in', 'great' etc., but never physically cold! When used in German it's inflected like any German adjective, including the comparative and superlative forms.

Das war 'n absolut cooles* Event*!

That was an absolutely cool event! [big events only, like a rock concert, the Queen visiting ...]

cooler* als das coolste* Gefährt

cooler than the coolest vehicle

The opposite exists as well: **uncool*,** whereby the **un-** is pronounced like traditional German! More Denglisch adjectives are for example: **over-/underdressed*, tricky*, trendy*, hip*, in*, stoned*, high*, spaced*...**

As for downloaden*:
The first approach follows the example of the correct German equivalent runtergeladen, *which is the past participle of the separable verb* runterladen (= ich lade die Datei runter).
The second approach recognises that you cannot actually separate the English word like that and therefore the past participle for non-separable verbs is formed.

German Dialects

This book cannot show all the dialect varieties of German colloquialisms, but concentrates on idiomatic language that has been in use for many years and will most likely continue to be used in German as if it were **Hochdeutsch** (standard German). However, even though the use of dialects is not as widespread as it used to be at the beginning of the 20th century, people will never cease to spice up their standard German with regional expressions. Let's therefore take a look at some of the regional dialects:

The north

The dominant north-western dialect is **Plattdüütsch (Plattdeutsch)** and is mostly spoken in the federal states Schleswig-Holstein, Lower Saxony, Hamburg and Bremen but also stretching into Mecklenburg - West Pomerania. In English it's usually referred to as Low Saxon or Low German.

Another dialect is Ostfriesisch, spoken in the north-west along the German North Sea coast and islands. East Frisian uses similar expressions as in Low Saxon, therefore I'll not crowd you with further examples.

In the northern federal states which were formerly in East Germany (especially in Saxony-Anhalt and Saxony) **Säggsch (Sächsisch)** is the primary dialect spoken. In English the dialect is called Upper Saxon.

Different again are the dialects in Mecklenburg - West Pomerania, Brandenburg and of course Berlin. **Berlinerisch (Berlinisch)** was voted to be the second most sexy German dialect in a survey by the German edition of the magazine Playboy (the most sexy one was Bavarian).

The south

The internationally best known German dialect is surely **Bairisch** (Bavarian). It's renowned for being spoken by women in bosom-displaying **Dirndl**-dresses and blokes in somewhat kinky **Lederhosen** (leather pants). Bavarian is used throughout Southern Germany in large parts of the federal state Bavaria, with the exception of the area around and north of Nuremberg **(Nürnberg)**, which is home to **Fränkisch.** Another variant of Bavarian is also at home in large parts of Austria.

In Vienna (Wien) *the people speak the special variant* Wienerisch.

The south-west of Germany on the other hand hosts Alemannic, or as they call it, **Alemannisch.** It can be found in the federal state of Baden-Württemberg, where it's called **Badisch,** but also in the French Alsace region **(Elsass)**, where it's known as **Elsässisch.** In the German speaking part of Switzerland it's called **Schwyzerdütsch (Schweizerdeutsch).**

The other dialect of the south-west is known as **Schwäbisch** which is used in the Swabian regions within the federal states of Bavaria and Baden-Württemberg.

The middle

The middle-west offers more than one dialect per federal state, probably because it's the most densely populated area of Germany: 18 million people live in North Rhine - Westphalia alone (530 persons/km²), speaking **Kölsch** in Cologne **(Köln)** and related Ripuarian Franconian dialects along the northern River Rhine from Bonn until the river disappears into the Netherlands.

The other bit of North Rhine - Westphalia is dominated by **Westfälisch,** called Westphalian in English, which is actually more closely related to Low Saxon again. It is also the home of coal miner's German, which is used in the **Ruhrpott** along the River Ruhr between Westphalia and the River Rhine. This area is the most densely populated region in the whole of Germany at almost 1.200 persons/km²! Not surprisingly newly invented idioms in this area tend to catch on easily in the rest of Germany.

The southern River Rhine region between Koblenz, the border with Luxemburg and Mainz on the River Main is home to both Moselle and Rhenish Franconian. It's spoken in the federal states of Rhineland-Palatinate **(Rheinland-Pfalz)** and Saarland. The dialect is subsequently called **Pfälzisch.** Another variant in the area is **Hessisch,** which is mainly spoken in the federal state of Hesse with Frankfurt at its heart.

Since the dialects of Berlin and regions in North Rhine -Westphalia have such a great influence on modern German idiom in sheer numbers already (one fourth of the total population), I've included some regional expressions from these.

Some examples in comparison

There are vast differences in greeting one another or expressing basic polite phrases. Since these are crucial to know, you will find the terms 'good day', 'how are you', 'goodbye', 'thank you' and 'sorry' listed for some German dialects:

	Good morning!	**Good day!**	**Good evening!**
Standard	**Guten Morgen!**	**Guten Tag!**	**Guten Abend!**
Plattdeutsch	*all times of day:*	**Moin moin!**	
Sächsisch	**Morschn!**	**Daach!**	**N'Abend.**
Berlinisch	**Morjen!**	**Tachchen!**	**N'Abend.**
Bairisch	*all times of day:*	**Grüaß God! / 'ß God! / Servus!**	
Zürichdialekt	*all times of day:*	**Gruezi! / Grüessech!**	
Badisch	*all times of day:*	**Sally! / Servus!**	
Schwäbisch	**Guada Morga!**	**Griaß Godd(le)!**	**Gudn Obnd!**
Kölsch	**Morjen!**	**Tach!**	**N'Abend.**
Westfälisch	**Moagen!**	**Tach(chen)!**	**N'Abend.**

There're certainly quite some differences and it's interesting to note that in some dialects, people prefer to not bother with different greetings (depending on the time of day) even though they could (e.g. in **Badisch: Gute Morge!** [*good morning*], **Gute Tag!** [*good day*] and **Gute Nobig!** [*good evening*], but they'll prefer **Sally!** and **Servus!**).

Even more pronounced are the dialect differences, when people embark on a conversation with one another and set out by asking after the other person's well-being:

Especially in the north, as of midday Germans tend to greet each other with **Mahlzeit!** [*mealtime*] *in a work situation, even though no-one may be eating at the time!*

You've probably heard that Germans mostly shake hands when greeting each other and only hug or kiss on the cheek when you've become very good friends.

	How are you?
Standard	**Wie geht's?**
Plattdeutsch	**Wie geiht?**
Sächsisch	**Wie gehdsn so?**
	Wie gehds dänne?
Berlinisch	**Wie jeht's?**
Bairisch	**Wie geht's?**
Zürichdialekt	**Wie gaht's?** *in Zürich*
Badisch	**Wie goat's da?**
Schwäbisch	**Wia gohd's?**
	Wia isch's oech?
Kölsch	**Wie jehd'et?**
Westfälisch	**Wie isset? Wie isses?**

	Goodbye!
Standard	**Tschüss.**
Plattdeutsch	**Adjüüs/Tschüüs.**
Sächsisch	**Dschissi.**
Bairisch	**Servus/Fürt di.**
Schwyzerdütsch	**Tschüss** in *Basel*, **Tschau** in *Zürich*, **Adie** in both
Badisch	**Tschau/Ade.**
Schwäbisch	**Ade/Adele/Tschissle!**
Kölsch	**Tschöö.**
Westfälisch	**Schüss! Schüssi! Tschau!**

These lists are by no means complete, but just help to get a bit of a feeling for the differences that can be expected.

	Thank you. You're welcome.
Standard	**Danke! Nichts zu danken.**
Plattdeutsch	**Danke! Da nich für.**
Sächsisch	**Danggscheen. Bittscheen.**
Bairisch	**Dankschä. Koa Ursach.**
Zürichdialekt	**Merci/Danke. Nöts danke.**
Badisch	**Merci/Dankschen. Scho recht.**
Schwäbisch	**Danggschee. Scho rächd.**
Westfälisch	**Danke. (Is) Schon okeh!**

	Sorry!
Standard	**Entschuldige/ Entschuldigung.**
Plattdeutsch	**Pardong/Tschülligung.**
Sächsisch	**Schuldjung/Schuldchnsä.**
Berlinerisch	**Entschuldjense.**
Zürichdialekt	**Exgüsi.**
Schwäbisch	**Tschuldichong.**
Badisch	**Tschuldigung.**
Westfälisch	**Schuldigung. Schuldige.**

Yes. Maybe. Sure.

With your smartphone you can listen to words, sentences and phrases from this chapter. Just use a QR code reader.

Bon = Quittung = *receipt*

paletti is a word of unclear origin. It's possibly the Italian plural for paletta, which is the painter's palette. It could then mean 'all is in order', as in 'I have all the colours'.

When asking for something, you'd hope for a straightforward answer. But to distinguish between 'yes' and 'no' is not always easy. There are many regional and personal preferences in the use of idioms.

Yeah, okay.

Especially among young people, a wide range of rather fancy expressions for 'yes' can be heard. One example being **gebongt,** which originates from **bongen** – formerly used to express that a sold item has been entered into the cash register and a receipt produced.

Other figurative idioms are **geritzt** [*carved*], **alles paletti** [*all fine*], **kein Thema** [*no topic*], **oki doki*** [*okeydoke*], **wird erledigt** [*will be done*] and **geschenkt** [*consider it a present*].

Standard ways would be **okay*/O.K.*/in Ordnung** [*okay*], **gern** [*with pleasure*], **abgemacht** [*agreed*] or **klar** [*clear*]. The latter can be softened to **klaro** and **logisch** [*logical*] to **logo.** These are somewhat tongue-in-cheek attempts to imitate Italians or Spanish.

The word **klar** can also be combined to the following play on words and sounds:

Klar wie Kloßbrühe/Klärchen/Tinte!
Crystal-clear!
[*clear like dumpling broth / little Clara / ink*]

Tja, an (und) für sich spricht nix dagegen.
Well, I can't think of a reason why not.
[well basically nothing speaks against that]

An (und) für sich literally means 'to (and) by itself' and is used to express 'basically'.

If asked to help with something you can express that you'll do it voluntarily:

Eh ich mich schlagen lasse!
You don't have to twist my arm, I'll do it!
[before I let myself be beaten (to do it)]

If a German meant to say 'understood' or 'right' he'd use Ach so!

If it took a lot of convincing, you would claim, that you had no choice, but to give in:

Ich hab mich nochmal breitschlagen lassen.
I let them talk me into it! [I have let myself (be) beaten into breadth once again]

When you need to express that a device is fully functional or simply suitable for the intended purpose, you may say:

Das Teil is' astrein in Ordnung.
That thing is perfectly alright.
[that part is perfectly okay]

The term astrein *literally means 'clear of branches' and refers to a perfect piece of wood.*

In a shared house for example, you could say this when rinsing not only your own dirty cup, but also those of the others:

Wennschon, dennschon!
Might as well, while I'm at it!
[if any, then all]

Maybe ...

Indecisive persons tend to go for none of the above and just choose any term to keep it at **vielleicht** *[maybe]*:

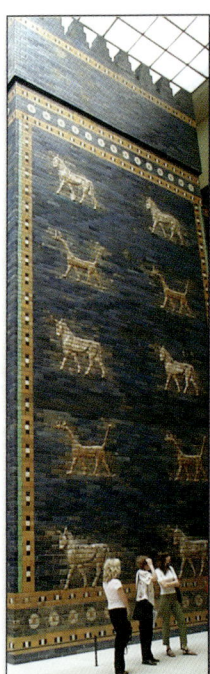

Mal gucken/schauen.	**Schauen wir mal!**
Maybe. (Wait and see.)	Wait and see.
Ich weiß noch nich'.	**Kann schon sein.**
I don't know yet.	Could be.
Kann hinhauen.	**Ich überleg's mir.**
Could be possible.	I'll think about it.
Möglich.	**Könnte sein.**
Possibly.	Could be.

A more amusing answer refers to a slogan coined by a TV advertisement for the German light beer Clausthaler in 1990:

Nich' immer, aber immer öfter.
[not always, but more and more often]

The origin of the next idiom is unknown, but it's based on the belief, that just about anything can be sorted out over a nice hot cup of tea. This implies that the phrase was coined up north which is traditionally inhabited by tea lovers (mostly black tea with milk and sugar as opposed to coffee drinkers down south):

Abwarten (und) Tee trinken.
Let's just wait and see. *[wait (and) drink tea]*

Promise!

Versprochen *[promised]* can be used to confirm that you'll do what you've been asked. You can also use **Hand drauf** or **ich schwöre,** which both mean 'I swear'. The first literally means: *'hand on it'*, as a reference to making an oath with one hand on the Bible.

Hand aufs Herz!
Cross my heart! *[hand on the heart]*

Großes (Indianer-)Ehrenwort!
I give you my word of honour.

The long version literally means *'great Indian word of honour'* as a reference to popular Wild West books and films.

Sure! Of course!

If doubts are uttered, you may want to confirm with reassurance that it can be done:

Wir werden das Kind schon schaukeln!
We'll manage!
[we'll rock the child (and stop it from crying)]

Simpler ways of saying 'sure' are: **gewiss** *[surely]*, **natürlich** *[naturally]*, **selbstverständlich** [goes without saying], **(aber) sicher (dat)** [sure] – the 'but' and 'that' often being added in the Cologne-region – and **freilich** [of course], which is very popular in the south.

Kannste dich drauf verlassen!
You can count on it!

If you prefer a Christian comment, you can 'proclaim':

In spoken German **Das's so sicher wie das Amen in der Kirche.**
'ist' is mostly reduced to As sure as the Pope is a Catholic!
a 'is' or even a mere [that is as certain as the amen in the church]
's' after a 'das'.

In medieval times your faith was tested by making you swallow a potion of **Gift** [poison]. Whoever dared to, took a leap of faith:

Da kannste Gift drauf nehmen!
You can bet on that!
[you can take poison on that]

Rather heathen are reassurances which refer to gambling activities and other things:

Lassen is short for ver- **Darauf könnt ich meinen Arsch verwetten!**
lassen = 'to count on so- I'd bet my balls on that!
mething'. [I could bet my arse on that]
Einen lassen können is a
humorous mixture with **Worauf du einen lassen kannst!**
einen fahren lassen, You can count on that!
which means 'to fart'! [you can let/count one on that]

No! No Need! As If!

The usual struggle for who pays the bill can be resolved by a friendly 'Come on, just leave it!' starting with **Komm, ...:**

... lass stecken! *[let (it) stick (in the pocket)]*
... lass gut sein! *[let (it) be good = let it go]*
... lass mal! *[let (it) once = leave it]*

If you politely want to decline any offer: **Nein danke. Nix für ungut! Ungut** literally translates into *'un-good'* and basically means 'no hard feelings'. Often offers are turned down due to pride. But if something is meant as consolation, even though nothing could possibly make up for the misfortune you've suffered, you'd literally say:

Dafür kann ich mir auch nix kaufen.
That won't get me anywhere either.
[I also cannot buy myself nothing for that]

It's not restricted to handling money. These idioms can also be used, when referring to other types of help offered.

Not interested!

For example, if a friend tries to convince you to go to the movies, but you really don't want to, these are typical comments to make:

Nein, kein Interesse! *[no interest]*
Nö, keine Lust! *[no desire]*
Nee, keinen/null Bock! *[no/nill buck/urge]*

No! No Need! As If!

As you can see,
there are quite some
ways to pronounce
a simple 'no'!

Nä, keine Böcke! *[no bucks (=urges)]*

Nä, keinen Nerv! *[no nerves]*

Nö, mir is' nich' danach (zumute).
[I'm not (in the mood) thereafter]

Das is' nich' so mein Ding.
That's not quite my cup of tea.
[that is not quite my thing]

Das is' nich' so meins.
That's not for me.

Don't feel like it!

You don't feel like going to yet another shop
after an extensive shopping spree:

Danke, mir reicht's!
I've had enough. *[thanks, it's sufficient for me]*

Danke, ich bin bedient.
That's enough for me, thanks. *[I am served]*

Danke, mein Bedarf is' gedeckt.
I've had it. *[my needs are covered]*

Nee danke, ich kann mich auch beherrschen.
No thanks, I can control myself.

Nee danke, ich kann mich gerade noch(mal) zurückhalten.
No thanks, I can't be bothered.
[I can once again just hold myself back]

Ich kann nich' aus meiner Haut.
I can't force myself to do that.
[I cannot (get) out of my skin]

Das kann ich nich' bringen/machen.
I can't bring myself to do that.
[I cannot bring/make that]

Beim bloßen Gedanken wird mir schon schlecht!
I feel sick just thinking about it!
[I feel already bad at the mere thought]

No problem!

When asked if something bothers you, you may answer referring to the little value of beans **(Bohnen)** which were used by children as play money in former times:

Nich' die Bohne.	**Nich' im geringsten.**
Not one bit.	Not the slightest bit.
Kein bisschen.	**Kein Problem.**
Not a bit.	No problem.

No! No Need! As If!

If you are asked to do something outrageous and you have no intention of complying, you can ward them off by saying:

Das wär ja noch schöner!
As if I would! *[that would be even nicer]*

All of the comments introduced in 'As If!' are expressed with great irony! In order to achieve this you need to stress the right bits in the sentence.

Da biste bei mir anner falschen Adresse!
You're barking up the wrong tree!
[you are at the wrong address at my place]

Wo denkste hin?!   **Ich denk nich' dran.**
What do you think?!   I don't think so!

Das fehlt gerade noch!
That's exactly what I need!

Und wenn du dich aufn Kopf stellst!
No matter what you do!
[and even if you put yourself on your head]

Da kannste lange warten!
You'll be waiting a while!

Da kannste warten, biste schwarz bist!
You can wait until judgement day!
[you can wait until you are black; refers to the colour of a decaying corpse]

If you are accused of having done something you simply did not do:

Das geht auf keine Kuhhaut!
That's incredible! *[that fits on no cow's skin]*

Davon kann keine Rede sein!
What makes you think that?
[thereof can be no talk]

Damit hab ich nix am Hut!
I don't do stuff like that!
also: I've got nothing to do with that.
[I have nothing of hat (=head/mind) with that]

Da kommt Freude auf.
I can hardly wait (ironically!)
[there arises joy]

To make clear that it's an impossible insinuation an idiom with Kuhhaut *[cow skin] is used. It refers to the belief in medieval times, that an ordinary person's list of sins should fit onto a sheep's skin. However, if the devil needs a cow's skin to list the sins, the list must be extraordinarily long!*

Great! Not Bad! Wow!

Outbursts of joy can be rather confusing, since this type of expression often has multiple connotations. If something is simply great, it's **cool*** (yes, the English word), **geil** *[cool!; also: hot/horny]*, **stark** *[striking/strong]*, **abgefahren** *[spectacular; also: drove off]*, **irre** *[insane]*, **abgedreht** *[bewildering; also: something turned off]*, **spitze** *[tops]*, **umwerfend** *[knock out]*, **dufte** *[great]*, **korrekt** *[correct]*, **optimal** *[optimal]*, **intergalaktisch gut** *[intergalactically good]*, **riesig** *[gigantic]* or **bombastisch** *[bombastic]* or **verschärft** *[hot; also: sharpened]* – to name a few.

Great! Not Bad! Wow!

Since Germans just love to emphasise, they combine **super-** *[super]*, **ultra-** *[ultra]*, **mega-** *[mega]*, **giga-** *[giga]*, **extrem** *[extremely]*, **echt** *[really]*, **voll** *[fully]*, **total** *[totally]*, **absolut** *[absolutely]*, **verdammt** *[damned]*, **einfach** *[simply]*, **höllisch** *[hellishly]* or **wahnsinnig** *[madly]* with the above to statements like **supergeil, ultracool*, echt irre, voll abgedreht, total spitze, verdammt abgefahren, einfach umwerfend ...** Something can also be **'ne Wucht** *[smashing!; also: a vehemence]*, **klasse** *[choice!; also: class]* or in teenager's terms **echt fett*** *[real phat; also really fat]*.

Real trendy stuff is **angesagt** *[hip; also: announced]* and **kultig** *[cult(y)]*, but also just like in English: **hip*, in*** and **trendy***.

Additionally, a small rhetorical grunt is often attached at the end of a sentence in order to seek the listener's approval:

Die sind jetzt voll angesagt, wa?!
That's really hip now, eh?

In German writing you'll often see '?!' which is used to stress the rhetoric quality of the statement. You'll also hear: **woll?!** in the Ruhr area and Westphalia, **nu?! / ne wa?!** in Saxony, **wa?!** in Berlin or Cologne, **gelletse?!** or **gell?!** in Swabia, **nidd?!** or **ned?!** in Hesse, **gell?!, nüd wahr?!** or **nöd?!** in Zürich, **gäu?!** in Bern, **nid wohr?!** or **nid?!** in Basel and **od'r?!** all over Switzerland. Between North Rhine - Westphalia and the north you'll also hear **ne?!** The little **ey** equals the affirmative 'just' and is used especially by the working class.

Das war voll cool*, ey! (pronounced: ääääj)
That was just so cool, eh!

Geil [hot/cool] and **stark** [striking] can also be combined with **affen-** [monkeys-], **oberaffen-** [alpha-monkeys] or the even funnier **oberaffentitten-** [alpha-monkeys-tits-], which is fashionable with teenagers in phrases like:

Das Video is' einfach oberaffengeil!
That video is just fucking awesome!

Affenstarke Performance*!
Bloody great performance!

Affengeile Tussi!
Top bird!/Hot babe!

A merger with a female member of the animal world is also quite popular: **sau-** [sow] can be heard in exclamations like **saugut** [sow good], expressing that it's 'incredibly good', or **saustark** [sow striking] to simply state any sort of amazement, as in 'wow'!

More combinations exist with **-mäßig** [-like] **saumäßig cool*** [sow-like cool], if more than just cool, **spitzenmäßig** [tops-like], if absolutely tops, **supermäßig stark** [super-like striking], if really something, **hammermäßig** [hammer-like] and also **hammerhart** [hammer hard], if just fab. **Allererste Sahne!** [very first cream] declares that something is the absolute best!

The exclamation wow* *itself is usually used in a positive sense, as are most of the expressions introduced in this chapter.*

Those which express astonishment with more mixed feelings are introduced in the section 'Really? Full On! Stunning!'.

Great! Not Bad! Wow!

Smooth!

The idiom 'it's all in butter' originally expressed that everything has been cooked with real butter and not with some cheap inferior grease.

Es is' alles in Butter.
Everything is okay.

Alles glatt gelaufen.
It all went smoothly.

Es läuft alles wie geritzt/geschmiert.
It's all running like clockwork.
[it all runs like carved/lubricated]

Es fluppt.
It's all going smoothly. *[it slides]*

Es läuft/klappt wie am Schnürchen.
It's going like clockwork.
[runs/works out like a little string]

Im grünen Bereich literally means 'in the green area' and refers to the green signal on any electronic device (such as voltmeters or traffic lights) indicating that there's no danger.

Es is' alles im grünen Bereich.
It's all under control.

Not bad, eh?

When in doubt or if you simply prefer a more modest reaction:

(Gar) Nich' verkehrt/übel/schlecht!
Not bad (at all).

Nicht zu verachten.
Nothing to complain about. *[not to disdain]*

Nich' von schlechten Eltern.
Nothing to be sneezed at.
[not from bad parents]

Nicht schlecht, Herr Specht.
[not bad mister woodpecker; which is merely an example of rhyming slang!]

Das hat was (für sich).
It's got something going for it.

Good at it!

Sie macht keine schlechte Figur!
She's not too bad at it! *[makes no bad figure]*

Er hat echt 'n Händchen dafür.
He's really good at it.
[he really has a little hand for it]

Der hat echt was aufm Kasten.
He really knows a thing or two.
[he really has some on the box (= head)]

Das liegt voll auf meiner Wellenlänge.
That's just on my wavelength.

Shit! No Good!

The notion of finding things awful, shitty, no good, too old or useless is traditionally expressed by calling it human or animal waste: **Scheiße** *[shit]*, **Mist** *[manure]*, **Dreck** *[dirt]* or **Kacke** *[crap]*. These terms can be used by themselves, just like **shit*** and **fuck*,** which are used in German as well.

The above as well as the noun **Shit*** and colourful synonymous expressions like **Hundekacke** *[dogs crap]*, **Hühnerkacke** *[chickens crap]*, **Müll** *[rubbish]*, **Schrott** *[junk]*, **Käse** *[cheese]* or **Scheißdreck** *[shit dirt]*, **Scheibenkleister** *[window glue]* can also be added to **Was für ein(e)/'n(e) ...** *[what a]*:

It's not clear why Käse is used as the equivalent to 'rubbish', but it may be related to the fact that cheese can have a very strong smell.

Was für eine/'ne Hühnerkacke!
What a bunch of crap!

The term Scheibenkleister evolved to disguise the use of the word Scheiße, especially when children are present.

To emphasise, **letzte** *[last]* or **allerletzte** *[very last]* may be added to any of the above:

Das is' doch der (aller-)letzte Schrott!
That's an absolute worthless piece of shit!
[that is just the (very) last junk]

Das is' doch das (Aller-)Letzte!
That's absolute crap! *[that's just the (very) last]*

Somewhat biblical expressions like **verdammt** *[damned]*, **verflucht** *[cursed]* and it's

softened version **verflixt** *[darned]* can be used
by themselves or combined:

(Was für 'ne) verdammte Scheiße!
God damn it! *[(what a) damned shit]*

So'n verfluchter Mist!
What a pain in the arse!

Verflucht/verdammt/verflixt nochmal!
Fucking hell!

Verdammt/verflixt und zugenäht!
Bloody hell!

*Zugenäht literally means 'sewn up'.
Of the three verflixt is the least blasphemic!*

Himmel, Arsch und Zwirn/Wolkenbruch!
For Christ's sake!
[heaven, arse and yarn/cloudburst]

Das is' doch gequirlte Scheiße!
What a piece of shit! *[that's just whisked shit]*

*Kruzitürken noch einmal! or its variation Kreuzkruzitürken can be used in anger or with astonishment in Bavaria. It's a phrase which has been around since the 16/17th century, when the Turks invaded Christian Europe.
Kruzi is short for Kruzifix = cross; and Türken = turks.*

Das is' doch unter aller Sau/Kanone!
That's bloody awful!
[that is just beneath all sows/cannons]

Das Teil is' (voll) im Arsch/Eimer!
That's (totally) fucked!
[that part is (fully) in the arse/bin]

Das is' doch/echt / voll fürn Arsch/Eimer!
What a bunch of crap!
[that is just/really fully for the arse/bin]

Shit! No Good!

There are so many ways to express that something is shitty, rubbish or simply fucked: **saumäßig** [sow-like], **ätzend** [corrosive = revolting], **assig** [antisocial], **abgefuckt*** [fucked off], **beschissen** [shitty], **miserabel** [miserable], **lausig** [lousy], **grottenschlecht** [grotto bad] and **mau** [pissweak].

If someone stuffed something up, it's **verpatzt** [snafu], **vergeigt** [played false on the violin], **verhauen** [hit wrongly], **vermasselt** [stuffed up], **vermurkst** [mucked up], **verbrezelt** [done with the wrong Pretzel], **verkorkst** [screwed up (the wrong cork)], **verpfuscht** [blundered] or **versaut** [messed up (like a sow)].

Same old shit!

Es is' (doch) immer nach demselben Muster gestrickt!
It's always the same old routine!
[it is (just) always knitted using the same pattern]

Es is' (doch) immer die alte Leier / das gleiche Lied!
It's always the same old story!
[it is (just) always the old lyre / the same song]

Das is' doch 'n alter Hut!
That's old hat! [that is just an old hat]
... kalter Kaffee!
That's old news! [cold coffee]
... Schnee von gestern!
That's yesterdays news! [snow from yesterday]

Plural is required for **Das sind (doch) alte/ olle Kamellen!** which doesn't refer to 'old caramels', but instead to 'old camomile' which has lost its healing effects.

Die Story* hat schon so'n Bart!
[the story has such a beard already]
Das is' doch von anno dazumal!
[that's just from the year of long gone days]
Das is' doch von anno Tobak!
[that's just from the year of tobacco]
Das is' doch Asbach Uralt!
[that's just Asbach ancient]
All mean: That's ancient history!

The last one is an amusing play on words mixing Asbach Uralt *(name of a famous brandy from* Rüdesheim *on the River Rhine) with the standalone meaning of* uralt *[ancient].*

The next three all mean: 'That's six of one and half a dozen of the other':

Das is' (doch) dasselbe in Grün!
[that is (just) the same in green]
... gehüpft wie gesprungen.
[hopped like jumped]
... Jacke wie Hose.
[jacket like pants]

Boring! Stupid!

Utter boredom is a good reason to complain: **(voll) öde** *[(fully) dreary]*, **dröge** *[dry]*, **gähnend langweilig** *[yawning boring]*, **lahm** *[lame]* or worse **arschlahm** *[arse lame]*.

Der is' so aufregend wie 'ne Schlaftablette!
He's as exciting as a wet week.
[he is as exciting as a sleeping pill]

Some German curses for persons can be used for males and females. The ending -in is for females and in other cases the ending on -r is for males. In this book the different endings are indicated.

A person who's dreadfully boring is a **Langweiler(in)** or a **Sesselpuper(in)** *[armchair pooper]*, because he or she doesn't do anything and just sits at home all day.

Of course things can simply be stupid as well: **doof** *[imbecile]*, **blöd** *[daft]*, **zu dumm** *[too dumb]*, **durchgeknallt** *[deranged]*, **beschränkt** *[limited]*, **irre** *[insane]*, **verrückt** *[crazy]*, **deppert** *[twitty]*, **behämmert** *[hammered on]*, **bescheuert** *[stupid]*, **bekloppt** *[wacked]*, **beknackt** *[nuts]*, **bestusst** *[nonsensical]*, **plemplem** *[loco]* or **affig** *[monkey-like]*.

Disgusting!

Ich krieg das kalte/große Kotzen!
It just makes you vomit!
[I get the cold/big puke]

Das is' doch zum Kotzen!
It just makes you sick to the stomach!
[that is just to (make you) puke]

Ich find dich zum Kotzen!
You make me sick!
[I find, you (make me) puke]

Das hängt mir echt zum Hals raus!
I'm absolutely fed up with it!
[that really hangs out of my throat]

Es kommt mir (schon) zu 'n Ohren raus!
I can't stand it any more!
[it comes out of my ears (already)]

Ich hab die Nase (gestrichen) voll (davon).
I've absolutely had it!
[I have the nose (level) full of it]

Hate it!

Ich hasse das wie die Pest!
I just hate it! *[I hate that like the plague]*

Ich kann's aufn Tod nich' ab!
I hate it with a passion!
[I can't stand it on the death]

Instead of **abkönnen** you can use **leiden können** *[to like]* or **ausstehen können** *[to stand].*

Note: leiden *all by itself means 'to suffer'.*

Da steh ich nich' drauf.
It's not my cup of tea. *[I don't stand on this]*

Das macht mich nich' an.
It doesn't grab me. *[that doesn't turn me on]*

Shit! No Good!

Forget about it!

Does the quality of the purchased item or the situation suck and you need to let off some steam? That's when you start out with **Das (Teil) kannste ...** *[you can ... that (part)]*:

... vergessen/knicken/abhaken!
[forget/bend/tick it]
... dir abschminken!
[demake-up it of yourself]
... in der Pfeife rauchen!
[smoke it in the pipe]
... in die Tonne kloppen/treten!
[knock/kick it in the barrel]
... dir in die Haare schmieren!
[smear it in your hair]
... dir an den Hut stecken!
[pin it to your hat]

Kiss My Arse! Who Cares!

Frustration levels rise. You just don't care anymore and choose to conclude rudely:

Das kannste dir in 'n Arsch schieben!
(You can) shove it up your arse!

Das (Teil) kannste dir sonstwohin stecken!
You can shove it where the sun doesn't shine!

sonstwohin literally means 'where else to'

Weißt du, wo du dir das hinstecken kannst?
You know where you can shove that?

Kiss my arse!

Leck mich (am Arsch)!
Kiss my arse! *[lick me (at the arse)]*

Du kannst mich mal (am Arsch lecken)!
You can kiss my arse!

Fick dich (ins Knie)!
Go fuck yourself! *[fuck yourself (in the knee)]*

Ich scheiß/pfeif auf dich.
Fuck you! Screw you! *[I shit/whistle on you]*

Who bloody cares?

Na und?!   **Was kümmert mich das?**
So what?   Why should I care?

47

Das is' nich' mein Bier!

That's nothing to do with me! *[that's not my beer (only my beer gets my attention)]*

Das geht mir am Arsch vorbei!

I can't be buggered/fucked! *[that goes passed my arse]*

'No rooster crows after that' means that if it's important enough, the rooster will crow! This refers to God's prophecy in the first evangelism of the New Testament: 'I tell you Peter, before the rooster crows you will have disowned me three times'. A prophecy which was fulfilled soon after Jesus was arrested.

Danach kräht doch kein Hahn!

Who bloody cares? *[no rooster crows after that]*

Scheiß (der Hund) drauf!

You can wipe your arse with it! *[shit (the dog) on it]*

Nach mir die Sintflut!

It doesn't matter what happens after I'm dead and gone! *[after me the deluge]*

Das kann mir gestohlen bleiben!

I couldn't care less! *[that can remain stolen to me]*

The phrase 'after me the deluge' was supposedly coined by the marquess of Pompadour after the battle at Roßbach in 1757.

Das tangiert mich nur peripher!

I don't care! *[that is tangential to me only peripherically]*

Wen juckt das schon?

Who gives a shit? *[who ever itches (from) that]*

Was kratzt mich das?

What do I care? *[what does that scratch me]*

Is' mir doch Wurs(ch)t!
I don't care! *[it is sausage to me]*

Instead of **Wurs(ch)t** you can also use **egal, schnuppe, schnurz, piepegal, schnurzpiepegal** *[all: whatever/all the same]* or **scheißegal** *[shit same]*. Great figures of speech are the following phrases for 'that's neither here nor there':

Das is' weder Fisch noch Fleisch.
[that is neither fish nor meat]
Das is' nix Halbes und nix Ganzes.
[that is nothing half and nothing whole]

Get stuffed!

These expressions can be used when someone has asked you to do something. But, you just won't do it.

Du kannst mich mal kreuzweise!
Kiss my arse! *[you can (lick my arse) crosswise]*

Du kannst mich gern haben!
You know what you can do!
[you can like me; ironically!]

Du kannst hingehen wo der Pfeffer wächst!
Go to hell! *[you can go where the pepper grows]*

Du kannst mir 'n Buckel runterrutschen!
Get lost! *[you can slide down my back]*

Whereas gern haben *generally means 'to like', in this case it's used ironically and means exactly the opposite: 'to hate', because you never want to see that person again.*

49

Really? Full On! Stunning!

With your smart-phone you can listen to words, sentences and phrases from this chapter.

In a conversation you can vary your comments of disbelief by throwing in:

Jetzt echt/ehrlich?
Really/Honestly?

Sag nich' sowas!
You don't say!

Mach keinen Scheiß!
You're kidding?!

Ohne Scheiß?
No shit?

Aber hallo!
Wow, really?

Oh Mann, ey!
Oh man! Blimey!

Mensch, das is' 'n Ding!
Wow! That's really something!
[man, that is a thing]

Der absolute/helle Wahnsinn!
Mad! Crazy!
[the absolute/bright madness]

Full on!

Some things have quite an impact, which is illustrated with words like **krass** *[crass]*, **derb** *[crude]*, **heftig** *[heavy]* as well as the English equivalents **heavy*** and **hardcore***.

Das is' ja wohl der Hammer/Hit*/Knüller!
That's absurd!
[that is surely just the hammer/hit/striker]

Really? Full On! Stunning!

Das is' doch die Härte!
That just about tops it! *[that's just the hardness]*

Der bringt Klöpse!
He does/says incredible stuff.
[he brings dumplings]

'He brings dumplings' is really synonymous for 'he comes up with big ones'.

Das is' wirklich 'n starkes Stück!
That's a bit much! *[that's really a strong piece]*

Das is' 'n dicker Hund!
You're kidding me?! *[that is a fat dog]*

'A fat dog' is a synonym for something out of the ordinary.

Ich wär fast aus 'n Latschen gekippt!
I didn't know what hit me!
[I would have almost toppled out of the slippers]

Stunning!

If you're lost for words, you can say **Ich fass es nich'!** *[I can't grasp it]*, **Ich glaub's nich'!** *[I can't believe it]*, **Das gibt's doch nich'!** *[that just doesn't exist]*, **Isses denn wahr?** *[is it true then]* or **Ich werd nich' mehr!** *[I will (get it) no more]* and its Bavarian equivalent **Do legst di nieder!** *[it makes you lie down]*.

The shortest one is Boah ey! *[wow].*

Dazu fällt mir echt nix mehr ein!
I really don't know what to say!
[for that, I remember really nothing any more]

Ich glaub, ich spinne!
I must be dreaming!

Spinnen literally means 'spin (weird thoughts)', which is similiar to the English 'to spin lies'. It originates in the drawing out and twisting of fibre into thread.

Really? Full On! Stunning!

Das glaubst du doch selber nich'!
I don't think you believe that yourself!

Ich kack ab!
Seriously?! *[I cack off = to die painfully]*

Ich krieg die Krise!
I'll have a fit! *[I get the crisis]*

Na, da biste baff, was?!   **Ja, sauber!**
You're baffled as well.   Yeah, right!

Da schnallst du ab!
I'm dumbstruck! *[you unfasten; so it really means to lose all understanding]*

There is a series of expressions starting out with 'I think I …', such as:

Ich denk, ich steh im Wald!
I must be dreaming!
[I think I stand in the forest]

Ich denk, mich küsst/knutscht 'n Elch!
I must be seeing things!
[I think I am kissed/snogged by an elk]

Ich denk/dachte, mich trifft der Schlag!
I didn't know what hit me!

Ich denk, mich tritt 'n Pferd!
It blows me away!
[I think I am kicked by a horse]

Really? Full On! Stunning!

Da machst du Augen, was?!
Can you believe it?

Da schlackerst du mit 'n Ohren, was?!
Unbelievable, isn't it?
[you wag with your ears, no?]

Da staunst du Bauklötze, was?!
Now you're stunned too?

Mir hat's komplett den Atem verschlagen.
It just took my breath away.

Instead of **den Atem** *[the breath]* you can also use **die Sprache** *[the language]*.

Jetzt bleibt dir wohl die Spucke weg?
And now what do you say?
[your saliva just stays away now]

Bauklötze = *toy building blocks; refers to the squarish static look on someone's face when they've been amazed.*

Really? Full On! Stunning!

One can also use all the other words for 'mouth' introduced later in the chapter 'Shut Up! Bigmouth! Spit It Out!'.

Kriegst du den Mund nich' auf?
Lost for words? *[don't you get the mouth open]*

Er kriegt die Kiemen nich' auseinander.
Has the cat got your tongue?
[he doesn't get the gills apart]

Jetzt biste platt, was?
You must be speechless?
[now you're flattened, no?]

For goodness sake!

Start out with **(Ach,) du ...** *[(oh,) you]*:

... liebes bisschen!
[dear bit]

... meine Fresse!
[my trap]

... dickes Ei/Ding!
[thick egg/thing]

... meine Güte!
[my goodness]

... lieber Himmel!
[dear heaven]

... grüne Neune!
[green nines]

... heiliger Strohsack!
[holy straw pallet]

... heiliger Bimbam!
[holy ding dong]

I don't buy it!

Das kriegen die doch eh nich' auf die Reihe!
They'll never get that right!
[they just never get that in the row]

Das kriegen die doch eh nich' gebacken!
They'll never pull that off!
[they just never get that baked]

Ich fress 'n Besen, wenn das stimmt.
I'll eat my hat, if that's true.
[I devour a broom if that is true]

Das halt ich fürn Gerücht!
I'll believe it when I see it!
[I take that is a rumour]

Das stimmt nie im Leben.
There's no way that's true.
[never in (my) life that's true]

Feel Great! Excited! Lucky Me!

Life is full of surprises. You may win in the lottery today and go bankrupt tomorrow. Some idioms for your state of happiness:

Feel great!

Mir geht's blendend/spitze!
I'm doing just great!
[it goes blinding/tops with me]

Ich fühl mich wie neugeboren.
I feel like new a man/woman.
[I feel like newly born]

With your smartphone you can listen to words, sentences and phrases from this chapter.

Feel Great! Excited! Lucky Me!

Er is' in seinem Element.
He's in his element.

Ich fühl mich wie 'n Fisch im Wasser.
[I feel like a fish in the water]

Ich fühl mich wie die Made im Speck.
[I feel like the maggot in the bacon]

The seventh heaven is described as the highest heaven in pre-christian apocryphal texts. It's where the angels and God himself live.

Ich fühl mich wie im siebten Himmel.
I'm on cloud nine! *[I feel like in seventh heaven]*

Ich fühl mich wie ausgewechselt.
I feel like a different person. *[... like exchanged]*

Ich bin fit wie 'n Turnschuh!
I feel as fit as a fiddle! *[I'm fit like a sneaker]*

Excited!

Du strahlst ja über alle vier Backen!
You're all smiles! *[you just radiate across all four (face + butt) cheeks]*

Ich könnt Bäume ausreißen!
I feel like I can do anything!
[I could rip up trees]

'Happy like a wren' refers to the cheerful song of this bird.

Ich freu mich wie 'n Schneekönig!
I'm as happy as a lark. *[I'm happy like a wren]*

Ich bin vollkommen ausm Häuschen!
I'm out of my mind with excitement!

Got lucky!

Schwein gehabt!
That was lucky! *[had pig; pigs bring luck]*

Um ein Haar!
That was a narrow escape! *[by one hair]*

Da haste ja nochmal Glück gehabt.
You were quite lucky there.

**Er hat für dich nochmal die Kastanien/
Kartoffeln ausm Feuer geholt.**
He saved your bacon.
[pulled your chestnuts/potatoes out of the fire]

Nochmal den Hals aus der Schlinge gezogen!
Escaped by the skin of my/your teeth!
[pulled the neck out of the (hangman's) rope]

This idiom is said to be based on a tale by La Fontaine, where a cat gets the chestnuts out of the fire for the monkey.

**Nochmal mit 'nem blauen Auge davonge-
kommen.**
Got off lightly there. *[got away with a blue eye
(black in English); implies that you could have
been hurt a lot worse]*

Ich hab gerade noch die Kurve gekriegt.
I barely scraped through.
[I have only just gotten (through) the curve]

'N blindes Huhn findet auch mal 'n Korn.
By the skin of your teeth.
[a blind hen also finds a grain sometimes]

Feel Great! Excited! Lucky Me!

Ich bin aus der größten Scheiße heraus.

I just managed to save my arse.

[I am out of the biggest shit]

Haste dich ja geschickt aus der Affäre gezogen!

You just managed to pull it off!

[you have just skilfully pulled yourself out of the (tricky) affair]

The idiom ausm Schneider *became popular because of its use in the card game* Skat *when getting 30 or 31 points. It refers to an old joke that a tailor* (Schneider) *weighs no more than 30 Lot = 30 g.*

Ich bin ausm Schneider.

I'm off the hook.

Da hab ich voll ins Schwarze getroffen.

I hit the bull's eye here.

Er hat echt den Vogel abgeschossen.

He outdid everybody. *[he really shot the bird; refers to shooting a bird off a stick at traditional shooting festivals]*

Exhausted! Wrong! Screwed Up!

The state of mind can be crucial for handling any situation in life. Someone who feels absolutely low may say:

Mir geht's dreckig/beschissen!
I feel like crap/shit! *[I am going dirty/shitty]*

Ich fühl mich (hunds)elend/bematscht!
I feel rotten! *[I feel (dog)miserable/mudded]*

Ich hab 'n Tief/'n Hänger.
I feel really low/down.

With your smartphone you can listen to words, sentences and phrases from this chapter.

Exhausted!

Ich bin vielleicht gerädert.
I'm really buggered.

Ich fühl mich wie durch'n Wolf gedreht.
I feel all wrung out.
[I feel like turned through a meat mincer]

Ich bin kaputt.
I'm knackered. *[broken]*

Kaputt can be substituted with **geschafft** *[exhausted]* or **fertig** *[finished]*. More playful is **fix und fertig** (a humorous combination for *'ready to use'*, which is a term used for instant meals), **fix und alle** (again a variation on the

Rädern refers to the medieval practice of killing a person by running over them with wheels and then tying the body to the wheel.

Wolf also means 'wolf', but it's an abbreviation of Fleischwolf (literally 'meat wolf') which is the term for 'meat mincer'.

previous) and last but not least, its amusing adaptation **fix und foxi** which happen to be the names of two comic book characters.

Your gums would be the last thing you have after loosing milk and adult teeth, especially if you wouldn't get any dentures.

Ich geh auf'm Zahnfleisch.
I'm at the end of my tether.
[I walk on my gums]

Ich weiß nich' wo mir der Kopf steht.
I've totally lost the plot.
[I don't know where stands my head]

Das schlaucht.
It wears me out. *[it tubes]*

You look terrible!

Du ziehst 'n Gesicht wie drei Tage Regen-wetter.
You look awfully sad!
[you pull a face like three days rainy weather]

Du siehst aus wie 'n Häufchen Elend.
You look miserable!
[you look like a little heap of misery]

Du siehst aus wie 'ne Leiche!
[you look like a corpse]

... 'n wandelnder Leichnam.
[a wandering corpse]
Both: You look like death warmed up!

Du siehst aus wie ausgelutscht!
You look like shit!
[you look like licked out]

Wie lange willste noch die beleidigte Leber-wurst spielen?
Must you always be in a huff?
[how long do you still want to play the offended paté/liverwurst]

The two idioms with Leber *(liver) are based on the old belief that the liver is the home of feelings (rather than the heart).*

Welche Laus is' dir denn über die Leber gelaufen?
What's eating you?
[which louse has run over your liver]

Steh nich' da wie 'n begossener Pudel.
Lighten up!
[don't stand there like a watered poodle]

It went wrong!

Das is' voll daneben gegangen!
That was a complete fuck-up/stuff-up!
[that has gone fully off/next-to-it]

Instead of daneben *you can use* in die Hose *[in the pants] or* in die Binsen *[in the rushes].*

Es ging komplett ins Auge.
It went completely wrong.
[it went completely in the eye = bad accident!]

Es is' schief gelaufen/gegangen.
It went wrong/pearshaped.
[it has run/gone crooked]

Exhausted! Wrong! Screwed Up!

Das war ja wohl 'n Schuss in 'n Ofen.
That was as useless as tits on a bull.
[that was surely just a shot in the oven]

Alles geht 'n Bach runter.
Everything goes straight down the drain.
[all goes down the creek]

Knapp vorbei is' auch daneben.
A miss is as good as a mile.
[getting close is also missed/off]

Screwed up!

**Das war wohl 'n Griff ins Klo /
in die Schüssel.** That was useless.
[that was just (like) reaching into the loo/bowl]

Ich könnt mich in den Arsch beißen.
I could kick myself.
[I could bite myself in the arse]

Holzweg is an agricultural term for 'access road ' which won't get you to another town.

Da war ich wohl auf'm Holzweg!
I was on the wrong track!
[I was just on the wood path]

Einen Bock schießen refers to the old custom that the worst shooter gets a buck as consolation price.

Da haste echt 'n Bock geschossen.
You cocked that one up!
[you have really shot a buck there]

Das is' nich' gerade die feine englische Art.
How rude!
[that's not exactly the refined English way]

Da hab ich mir nur ins eigene Fleisch geschnitten.
I've only just screwed myself.
[I have only cut myself in my own meat there]

Bad luck!

Dumm gelaufen!
Well, too bad! *[went dumb]*

Pech, der Zug is' abgefahren!
Bad luck, you missed the boat!
[bad luck, the train has driven off]

Ich hab wieder die Arschkarte gezogen.
I got the wrong end of the stick again.
[I have drawn the arse card again]

Voll in den Arsch gekniffen!
Bad luck! *[fully pinched in the arse]*

In deep shit!

Ihm reicht das Wasser bis zum Hals!
He's in over his head!
[the water reaches up to his neck]

Ihm steht die Scheiße bis zur Halskrause!
He's in deep shit. *[the shit rises up to his ruff]*

Du sitzt ganz schön in der Tinte.
You're really in for it.
[you sit pretty much in the ink]

63

Da siehst du aber alt aus!
You're really in for it. *[you look indeed old there]*

Der is' weg vom Fenster.
He's out of the running.
[he is gone from the window]

Ich bin geliefert.
I'm at the end of my rope. *[I am delivered]*

Da is' Hopfen und Malz verloren.
It's a lost cause.
[hops and malt are lost there]

Es is' zum Heulen/Mäusemelken!
It's hopeless!
[it is to (make you) cry / to milk mice]

At your wits' end.

Ich häng echt total neben der Spur.
I can't get myself together.
[I really hang next to the rails]

Ich bin (mit meinem Latein) am Ende.
I'm at my wits' end.
[I am at the end (with my Latin)]

Latin is synonymous for knowledge!

Ich krieg einfach kein Bein auf die Erde.
I can't get back back on my feet.
[I simply get no leg on the earth]

Hilarious! Joke! Fooled!

Life can also be a total blast and then there is no holding back:

Sie amüsierten sich köstlich.
They were having fun.
[they amused themselves deliciously]

Sie waren alle am Geiern/Grölen.
They were laughing their heads off.
[they were all vulturing/hollering]

If the laugh gets quite loud, it's **wiehern** [neigh], **schallend lachen** [to laugh clangorously] or **brüllen vor Lachen** [scream of laughter].

Instead of **brüllen vor Lachen** you can use the following verbs in front of **vor Lachen: sich biegen** *[to bend oneself]*, **sich kringeln** *[to bend oneself into a circle]*, **sich kugeln** *[to bend into a ball]*, **sich wegschmeißen** *[to throw oneself away]*, **sich ausschütten** *[to pour oneself out]*, **prusten** *[to snort]*, **platzen** *[to burst]* and more complex is **sich vor Lachen in die Hose machen** *[to piss one's pants laughing]*.

beömmeln or *beoemmeln is a typical expression in Ruhr-dialect.*

Ich hab mich total begeiert/beömmelt.
I had a good laugh.
[I have totally vultured/laughed]

Ich lach mich krumm.
What a laugh! *[I laugh myself bent]*

Instead of **krumm** *[bent]* you can also use **kringelig** *[squiggly]*, **schlapp** *[weak]*, **tot** *[dead]*, **krank** *[sick]*, **kaputt** *[broken]*, **schief** *[crooked]*, **krumm und schief** *[bent and crooked]*, **scheckig** *[spotted]* or **mir 'n Ast ab** *[laugh off a branch of myself]*.

If you are wondering, what on earth 'a branch' has to do with laughter: Well Ast used to be synonymous with 'back' and therefore refers to the image of a person bending forward with laughter again.

Ich konnt mich nich' mehr halten.
There was no holding back.

Er prustete los or: **brach in Gelächter aus.**
He burst out laughing.
[he snort out or: burst out in laughter]

Es is' zum Totlachen/Schießen/Brüllen!
It's so funny! *[it's to laugh-to-death/shoot/roar]*

More modest is to giggle, which is called **ki-chern** or less often **gicksen.** Before that happens the person may only be grinning, which is **grinsen** or **schmunzeln.**

Du grinst wie 'n Honigkuchenpferd.
You grin like a Cheshire cat.
[you grin like a honey cake horse]

This idiom may refer to gingerbread cookies baked in the shape of horses and hung from the Christmas tree with jolly faces painted on them with sugar glazing.

All because it was just bloody hilarious: **komisch** [comical], **urkomisch** [fundamentally comical], **witzig** [amusing] or even **aberwitzig** [but still amusing] meaning ludicrous, **lustig** [funny] or **oberlustig** [top funny]. Someone's looks may cause all that laughter:

Du siehst zum Schießen aus!
You look ridiculous! [look to shoot]

Fooled!

Talented funny daddies can make a fool of you. This is how you accuse them of it:

Verarschen kann ich mich selber/alleine.
I don't need you to make me look like an arse. [I can arse myself alone]

Instead of **verarschen** you can use **verscheißern** [to shit on], **verkohlen** [to char], **veräppeln** [to apple on], **vergackeiern** [to funny egg], **betuppen** [to deceive; Ruhr dialect] and **anschmieren** [to smear on].

veräppeln refers to Pferdeäppel *(horse apples)* = horse shit

Hilarious! Joke! Fooled!

Ich hab doch Augen im Kopf!
I'm not blind! *[but I have eyes in my head]*

Du willst mich wohl aufn Arm nehmen?
You're pulling my leg, aren't you?
[you just want to take me on the arm]

... mich wohl zum Narren halten?
[you just want to take me for a fool]
... mir wohl 'n Bären aufbinden?
[you just want to tie a bear onto me]
... mir wohl 'n X für 'n U vormachen?
[you just want to present me an X for a U]

Die haben mich angeschmiert.
They fooled me. *[they have smeared on me]*

... mich aufs Korn genommen.
... conned me.
[taken me on the front of the gun]

Strich und Faden *refers* **... mich nach Strich und Faden verarscht.**
to a weaving style and ... strung me along.
type of weaving materi- *[fooled me by stripe and thread]*
al, which both need to **... mich aufs Glatteis geführt.**
be excellent ... led me up the garden path.
in order to sell well. *[led me onto slippery ice]*
... mich für dumm verkauft.
... took the piss out of me.
[sold me for dumb]
... mich ganz schön angeschissen.
... bullshitted me.
[pretty much shit at me]

... mich anner Nase rumgeführt.
... tricked me.
[led me around by the nose]

... mich auf die Schippe genommen.
... took the mickey out of me.
[taken me on the shovel]

... mich übern Tisch gezogen.
... put one over on me.
[pulled me over the table]

... mich aufs Kreuz gelegt.
... messed around with me.
[layed me on the back/spine]

Nonsense! Huh? No Clue!

Any type of nonsense can be labelled **Blödsinn** *[daft sense]*, **Humbug** *[humbug]*, **Kokolores** *[cockalorum]*, **Müll** *[rubbish]*, **Scheiße** *[shit]*, **Mist** *[manure]*, **Kacke** *[cack]*, **Schrott** *[junk]*, **Quatsch** *[blather]*, **Quark** *[soft curd cheese]*, **Pipikram** *[pissy small stuff]*, **Stuss** *[bullshit in Yiddish]*, **Schmu** *[talk]* or you use **Nonsens*** *[nonsense]*!

With your smartphone you can listen to words, sentences and phrases from this chapter.

Das is' doch voll Banane/daneben!
That's just crap!
[that's just fully banana/off]

Is' doch alles Mumpitz/Kappes/Pipifax!
Bullshit!
[is all just bullshit/cabbage/nitty gritty]

Da lachen ja die Hühner!
No-one can take that seriously.
[even the chickens laugh there]

Instead of Märchen
you can also use Am-
menmärchen,
*which literally means
'wet nurse fairy tale',
meaning
'old wives' tales'*

Erzähl doch keine Märchen!
Tell that to the marines!
[just tell no fairy tales]

Schluss mit den Sperenzkes!
Cut the crap!

Das is' doch an den Haaren herbeigezogen!
That's just absurd!
[that's just pulled in by the hair]

Instead of
den Sperenzkes *you can
also insert* dem Spökes
or den Fisimatenten.

Das is' doch 'ne fixe Idee von dir!
The very idea! *[that's just a fixed idea of yours]*

*More phrases for utter
disbelief have already
been introduced in the
chapter 'Really? Full
On! Stunning!'*

Jetzt komm mir nich' auf die Tour!
Don't bullshit me!
[now don't come to me in that way]

Du hast echt nur Scheiße im Kopf/Kopp.
You're full of shit.
[you really only have shit in your head]

Any stupid idea can be dismissed with **hirnrissig** *[brain cracked]* or **hirnverbrannt** *[brain
burned]*, both meaning 'daft'.

Hä?! Was is' denn jetzt kaputt?!
What's the matter now?
[huh? what's broken now then?]

I don't get it!

Das hab ich nich' gecheckt*.
I didn't get that.

Gecheckt* can be substituted with **ge-schnallt** [strapped], **kapiert** [grasped], **gerafft** [ruffled] and its slangy deformation **gerallt, gepeilt** [marine: sounded].

checken* *actually derives from the English word 'to check' and took on the meaning 'comprehend' in German.*

Ich schnall gar nix mehr!
I don't get it any more!
[I strap nothing (in my brain) any more]

Ich versteh immer nur Bahnhof!
It's as clear as mud to me!
[I always understand only (the word) station]

Ich blick's echt nich' mehr!
I don't get it any more!
[I really see it no more]

Da blick ich nich' durch.
I can't get the hang of it.
[I look not through that]

Ich hab keinen Durchblick mehr.
I'm lost here.
[I have no view any more]

Das is' mir zu hoch.
That's beyond me.
[that is too high for me]

Ich hab wohl 'n Brett vorm Kopf.
I must have blinkers on.
[I must have a board in front of the head]

Das will mir nich' in den Kopf.
It's over my head. *[that doesn't want in my head]*

To make fun of those who just don't get it:

'N bisschen schwer von Begriff/Kapee?
A bit slow? *[a bit difficult for understanding]*

Mann, hast du 'ne lange Leitung!
You're rather slow on the uptake!
[man, you have a long pipe]

No clue!

Woher soll ich das wissen?   **Keinen Plan!**
How should I know?   No idea!

Da bin ich überfragt.
I don't have a clue! *[I'm over asked there]*

Keine Ahnung!
No idea! *[no premonition]*

Keinen Blassen/Schimmer!
[no bleak one/glimmer]

Ich hab nich' die leisteste Ahnung!
I don't have the faintest idea!
[I don't have the most silent premonition]

Du hast von Tuten und Blasen keine Ahnung!
You don't know anything!
[you have no idea of toot and blow]

Ich tappe im Dunkeln.
I'm in the dark here. *[I grope in the dark]*

Du stehst wohl auf'm Schlauch!
You've only got one oar in the water!
[you just stand on the hose]

Weiß der Henker!
God knows! *[knows the hangman]*

You can also substitute the hangman with these: **der Himmel** *[heaven]*, **der Teufel** *[devil]*, **der Geier** *[vulture]* and **der Kuckuck** *[cuckoo]*.

Even a child can at least make a brass instrument toot.
A skilful person 'blows' nice tunes on the instrument. A poor bugger who has no idea of Tuten and Blasen *can't do either.*

Chat, Gossip & Whinge

The mouth is a great thing. It can be used for eating, drinking, kissing and talking. When the latter gets somewhat excessive, it's referred to as **labern** *[to prattle]*, **sülzen** *[to babble]*, **schwatzen** *[to rattle]* or **strunzen** *[to gabble]*. Accordingly, the talk itself is called **Gelaber** *[prattle]*, **Gesülze** *[babble]*, **Geschwätz** *[rattling]* or **Gesabber** *[drivel]*.

Jetzt texte mich nich' zu!
I don't want to hear it!
[now don't text me closed/full]

Laber mich nich' voll!
I'm not interested in your talk.
[don't prattle me full]

Instead of Driss, *which is used only in the northern Rhine area, you can again use all the words for 'rubbish' and 'shit' introduced earlier:* Müll, Scheiß, Kacke, Schrott, Mist, Quark ...

Laber keinen Driss!
Stop talking rubbish! *[prattle no bullshit]*

Chatterboxes are called **Labertasche** *[prattle bag]*, **Plaudertasche** *[chat bag]*, **Quasselstrippe** *[twaddle strip]*, **Quatschkopf** *[blather head]* and **alter Schwätzer(in)** *[old rattler]*. People who make excessive use of long and complicated words are known as a **Phrasendrescher(in)** *[phrase thresher]*.

If there is a feel of sensationalism: Schaumschläger(in) *[foam beater].*

Once the noise level resembles a flock of ducks, it's more **schnattern** *[to chatter]* or **quaken** *[to quack]*. And this can be turned into nouns as well: **Geschnatter** *[chatter]* and **Gequake** *[quack]*.

Ich kann das Gequake nich' mehr hören.
I'm sick of that chattering.
[I can hear that chatter no more]

Chat

The more casual chat occurs when engaging in **plaudern** *[to chat]*, **plauschen** *[to chitchat]*, **quatschen** *[to blather]*, **quasseln** *[to twaddle]* or **klönen** *[to twiddle]*.

Wir haben mal wieder so richtig geklönt.
We had a good chat again.

Wir hatten 'n schönes Plauderstündchen.
We had a nice little chit-chat.
[we had a nice little chat hour]

Wir kamen von Hölzchen auf Stöckchen.
We chatted about this and that.
[we came from little wooden pieces to little sticks]

The phrase von Hölzchen auf Stöckchen *really implies that all that talk was really about similar things and in the end nothing was important: Much ado about nothing!*

Tell me!

Revealing or telling someone something special is preferably done with **verticken** (also means 'to sell'), **verklickern** and **verzählen** (corruption of **erzählen** in river Rhine area).

In Westphalia this expression is pronounced like Höckschen auf Stöckschen *or* Höcksken auf Stöcksken! *Take your pick.*

Verzähl, was's los?
Tell me, what's the matter?
[tell, what's loose]

Das muss ich dir ja nich' gerade stecken.
As if I would tell you.
[I must not exactly stick you that]

Das muss ich dir ja nich' auf die Nase binden.
That's not for you to know.
[I must not tie you that on the nose]

Das muss ich dir ja nich' gerade unter die Nase reiben.
If I told you, I'd have to kill you!
[I must not exactly rub it under your nose]

Chat, Gossip & Whinge

This phrase really means that all that talk is hardly important or true for that matter.

Der redet viel, wenn der Tag lang is'.
He can't stop talking.
[he talks much when the day is long]

Sie redet wie 'n Wasserfall.
She just goes on and on.
[she talks like a waterfall]

Sie plaudert mal wieder ausm Nähkästchen.
She's shooting her mouth off again.
[she chats from the little sewing box once again]

Ich red mir hier den Mund fusselig.
I was talking until I was blue in the face.
[I talk my mouth fluffy here]

Quatsch keine Opern!
Can you just shut up? *[blather no opera]*

Jetzt kau mir kein Ohr ab!
(Why don't you) put a sock in it?!
[chew no ear off me now]

Kannste nich' wen anders zu-/volltexten?
Can't you dump that on someone else?
[can't you text closed/full someone else]

If the topics are mainly nonsensical, the preferred terms are: **faseln** *[to maunder]*, **sabbeln** *[to drool]*, **blubbern** *[to bubble]*, **plappern** *[to blabber]*, **schwafeln** *[to waffle]*, **schwallen** *[to* *yak]* and very idiomatically **dummschwallen** *[to dumb yak].* Some matching nouns are **Gefasel** *[maundering],* **Gesabbel** *[drool],* **Geschwafel** *[waffle],* **Geschwalle** *[yak],* **Geblubber** *[bubbling],* **Geplapper** *[blabber].* The person doing it is a **Dummschwätzer(in)** *[dumb rattler].*

You can also use the expressions equalling the term 'nonsense' which were introduced in the chapter 'Nonsense! Huh? No Clue!'.

Bei dem Geblubber kann man nich' ernst bleiben.
You can't keep a straight face around such blabbing.

Die faseln sich einen Müll zusammen.
They're talking rubbish.
[they maunder a rubbish together for themselves]

Das muss man ja auch nich' für bare Münze nehmen!
You don't have to believe everything you hear!
[one must also not take that for cash coins either]

You can tell them to tell their tales elsewhere and say 'don't bullshit me' like this:

Du kannst mir viel erzählen.
[you can tell me much]
Du kannst mir einen vom Pferd erzählen.
[you can tell me one about the horse]
Das kannste 'nem anderen erzählen.
[you can tell that someone else]
Das kannste deiner Großmutter erzählen.
[you can tell that your grandmother]

Gossip.

The chat turns into gossip, which is known as **klatschen** [to clap], **tratschen** [to gossip] and **lästern** [to blaspheme]. The person doing it is called **Tratschtüte** [gossip bag], **Klatschtante** [clap aunt], **Lästermaul** [blaspheme muzzle] or **Lästerzunge** [blaspheme tongue].

Sie ziehen ihn ständig durch 'n Dreck.
[they persistently pull him through the dirt]
Sie ziehen ihn ständig durch 'n Kakao.
[they persistently pull him through the cocoa]
Sie ziehen ständig über ihn her.
[they persistently bag (over) him]
All: They're always slagging him off.

über jemand herziehen also contains the word 'ziehen' (meaning 'pull'), but in this combination it only means 'to bag someone'

Sie machen ihn ständig fertig/schlecht.
They keep putting him down.
[they persistently finish him / make him bad]

Man zerreißt sich das Maul über sie.
They are bad-mouthing her.
[one tears its muzzle apart about her]

Nag, nag.

More of a monologue is whinging, which is known in German as **meckern** *[to bleat]*, **nörgeln** *[to nag]*, the North German **nölen** *[to whine]* and furthermore: **maulen** *[to moan]*, **mosern** *[to gripe]* and **zetern** *[to clamour]*, which can get really loud.

The person doing it is a **Meckerziege** *[bleat goat]* or **Meckerkuh** *[bleat cow]*.

Ich ertrag das Gezeter/Genörgel nich' mehr!
I can't stand all that nagging any more!

Die ständige Nörgelei is' unerträglich.
That constant nagging is unbearable.

Jetzt zick nich' so rum!
Now stop that bitching!
[now don't nanny-goat around like that]

Once the nagging gets an unfriendly feel to it and is directed against you, this is what you call **(blöd) anmachen** *[to (daftly) offend]*, **anpampen** *[to dis]* or **anprollen** *[to affront]*. Once it gets really insulting:

In a different context, anmachen *also means 'to come on to someone'.*

Hör auf zu stänkern!
Don't make a big stink! *[stop the stinking]*

Sie gab ständig pampige Antworten.
She kept giving bitchy replies/answers.
[she persistently gave stroppy answers]

Shut Up! Bigmouth! Spit It Out!

If you're generally annoyed with all that talk, whingeing, whining or hollering, you can command the person to just shut up. In German this is usually said involving various synonyms for 'holding your mouth':

The variation with -n (Goschen) is typically Bavarian or Austrian.

Halt die Klappe/Fresse/Gosche(n)!
Shut up! *[hold the trap/gob/yap]*

Halt einfach den Mund!   **Halt's Maul!**
Just keep your mouth shut! Shut your trap!

Jetzt halt verdammt nochmal den Schnabel!
Shut the fuck up! *[damn it, hold the beak now]*

Schnauze!   **Ruhe auf den billigen Plätzen!**
[snout]   *[silence on the cheap seats]*
Shut up!   Silence!

Bigmouth!

If someone's bragging a lot, you use any of the above words for 'mouth' and substitute its article with a combination of **dein** *[your]* and **groß** *[big]*: **Halt dein großes Maul! ... deinen großen Mund, ... deinen großen Schnabel** etc.

Note: One can't combine with Gosche(n)!

Jetzt mach aber mal halblang!
Come on, pipe down! *[make it half long now]*

Jetzt bleib aber mal aufm Teppich!
Come on, don't get carried away!
[just once stay on the carpet now]

Jetzt halt mal die Luft an!
Put a sock in it! *[hold the breath once now]*

A bragging person is a **Angeber(in)** *[bragger]*, **Aufschneider(in)** *[cock-a-doodle-doo]*, **Großkotz** *[big puke]*, **Großmaul** *[big muzzle]*, **Wichtigtuer(in)** *[important doer]*, **Schlaumeier(in)** *[clever dick]*, **Prahlhans** *[boast Hans]*, **Besserwisser(in)** *[better knower]* or **Klugscheißer(in)** *[smart shitter]*.

As you probably know, Meier is a very common German surname, whose origin is the Middle High German word meiger, which is the comparative degree for magnus (meaning 'the greater'). This term was used to describe farmers whose task was to look after a farm, in the name of their landlord.

Immer muss er den großen Mann markieren!
He's always throwing his weight around.
[he always must make out (to be) the big man]

Instead of **großen Mann** you can use **Max, Macker** *[bloke/leader]* and **Obermacker** *[top bloke/leader]*.

Immer muss er Sprüche klopfen!
He's always boasting.
[he must always knock sayings]

Der hat eine große Klappe/Fresse!
He's got a real big mouth!

Any term for 'mouth' from this chapter can be used in the phrase 'He's got a real big mouth!'.

Große Klappe, nix dahinter!
Big mouth, nothing behind it.
[big trap, nothing behind it]

Shut Up! Bigmouth! Spit It Out!

Aber das Maul aufreißen, das kannste?
You're all talk, aren't you?
[but rip open the mouth, that you can (do)?]

Aber 'ne dicke Lippe riskieren, was?!
You're a bit up yourself, aren't you?
[but risk a big lip, yes?]

This term refers to the somewhat overdone make up.
Du brauchst gar nich' so dick aufzutragen!
No need to lay it on so thick!
[you needn't to apply (it) so thick at all]

Immer muss er einen auf obercool* machen.
He's always making out to be supercool!

Spit it out!

Blatt vor den Mund refers to the old practice by actors to use thin masks in front of their faces, when saying something offensive. That way it could not be held against them, since anyone could have said it. Noone could see it was that particular actor!
Du musst kein Blatt vor den Mund nehmen.
You don't have to mince your words.
[you mustn't take a leaf before the mouth]

Rück schon raus mit der Sprache!
Come on, spit it out!
[just move out with the language]

Red nich' länger drum rum!
Get to the point!
[don't talk around it (any) longer]

Red nich' länger um den heißen Brei rum!
Don't keep beating around the bush!
[don't talk around the hot porridge (any) longer]

**Schleich nich' rum wie die Katze
um den heißen Brei!**

Don't pussy-foot around, just tell me!
*[don't prowl about like the pussy around the hot
porridge]*

Red einfach frei von der Leber weg.

Just speak your mind.
[simply talk free from the liver]

*And again,
the liver is thought
to be home to one's fee-
lings …*

Red mal Klartext/Tacheles!

Just give it to me straight!
[talk clear text once]

Komm mal zur Sache!

Just get to the point!
[come to the matter once]

Spuck's aus!

Spit it out!

Crazy! Driving Me Nuts!

All that talk from a **Nervensäge** *[nerve saw
= pain in the neck]* is affecting your peace of
mind and you have to vent your anger:

Das is' voll nervig!

That really/bloody annoying!
[that's fully nerve-racking]

Du nervst (total)!

You annoy me (bigtime)!

Crazy! Driving Me Nuts!

Du gehst mir auf die Nerven/Eier!
You get on my nerves!
[you get on my nerves/eggs(=balls)]

Instead you can conclude **Du gehst mir aufn ...** with **Wecker** *[alarm clock]*, **Zeiger** *[pointer]*, **Senkel** *[shoe lace]*, **Sack** *[sack/scrotum]*, **Sender** *[transmitter]*, **Geist** *[spirit]* or **Keks** *[biscuit/cookie]*.

Du raubst mir echt den letzten Nerv!
You annoy the shit out of me!
[you really steal my last nerve]

Du machst mich ganz hibbelig!
You make me nervous.
[you make me completely jumpy]

A nice analogy to flat tyres: **Ich bin vollkommen mit den Nerven runter!**
My nerves are really fried!
[I'm entirely down with the nerves]

Meine Nerven liegen blank!
I'm a wreck! *[my nerves lay bare]*

In the end, things may make you go crazy: **Es macht mich ganz verrückt/irre!**
It drives me insane!

The little word **irre** can be varied into **kirre** and implies getting confused:

Du machst mich ganz kirre!
You are messing with my head!

Crazy! Mad! Insane!

Du hast wohl 'ne Schraube locker?!
Have you got a screw loose?

Du hast doch/ja 'ne Meise / 'nen Vogel!
You are nuts! *[you just have a tit/bird]*

Either way, if you take the rhetorical approach or just a straightforward accusation, after the **Du hast wohl/doch/ja ...**, any of these work:

... einen anner Waffel/Klatsche!
[one at the waffle/swat]
... 'n Sprung in der Schüssel!
[a chip in the bowl]
... 'n Dachschaden/Knall!
[a roof damage/bang]
... 'n Schuss/Hau (weg)!
[a shot/hit (away)]
... 'ne Macke!
[a kink/defect]
... 'n Rad ab!
[a wheel off]
... den Arsch offen!
[the arse open]
... nich' mehr alle Tassen im Schrank!
[not all cups in the cupboard any more]
... nich' mehr alle Latten am Zaun!
[not all slats at the fence any more]
... nich' mehr alle (beisammen)!
[not all (together) any more]

All these examples can simply be translated as 'You are nuts!'.

Crazy! Driving Me Nuts!

Du bist wohl nich' ganz richtig im Kopf!
You're not quite right in your head!

In all of these examples wohl *[just/may/well],* doch *[just] and* ja *[surely] or* ja wohl *[surely just] can be used for additional exclamation.*

The exact same can be expressed by substituting **im Kopf** with **im Oberstübchen,** which literally means *'in the little room in the top of the house'.* You can also use **in der Birne** *[in the pear]*. After **Du bist (ja) wohl ...** you can say:

... nich' ganz gescheit!
[not entirely clever]
... nich' ganz bei Trost!
[not entirely at wit]
... nich' ganz bei dir!
[not entirely in you]
... nich' ganz dicht!
[not entirely sealed]
... von allen guten Geistern verlassen!
[left by all good ghosts]
... (total) durchgeknallt/beschränkt/irre!
[(totally) deranged/limited/insane]
... (total) verrückt/deppert/behämmert!
[(totally) crazy/twitty/hammered on]
... (total) bescheuert/bekloppt/beknackt!
[(totally) stupid/wacked/nuts]

Remember: Spinnen *literally means* **... (total) plemplem/gaga/meschugge!**

'spin (weird thoughts)', *[(totally) loco/gaga/meshuga]*
which is similiar to the English 'to spin lies'.
It originates in the drawing out and twisting of fibre into thread.

Bei dir hakt's doch!
You're crazy! *[it just got stuck in you]*

Du spinnst doch!
You're insane! *[you just spin]*

Tickste noch ganz richtig?!
Are you out of your mind?
[do you tick completely right]

Aber sonst geht's dir gut, ja?!
[but otherwise you are going fine, yes?]

Aber sonst geht's danke?!
You're perfectly alright apart from that?
[but otherwise it's thanks?]

Furious! Enough!

There's always a limit as to how much one can take, before the blood rises to a boil.

Die is' echt total/irre/wahnsinnig sauer!
She's totally/really pissed off!
[she is really totally/insanely/madly sour

Also possible are **stinksauer** *[stink sour]*, **stocksauer** *[stick sour]*, **fuchsteufelswild** *[fox devil wild]*, **vergrätzt** *[upset]*, **geladen** *[loaded]* or **außer sich** *[beside herself]*.

Ich hab 'ne Stinkwut!
I'm furious! *[I have a stink fury]*

Er schäumt vor Wut.
He seethes with rage. *[he foams with rage]*

Furious! Enough!

Ich hab echt so'n Hals!
I'm so angry! *[I really have such a neck]*

Ich ärger mich zu Tode!
I'm so damned angry! *[I anger myself to death]*

After **Ich ärger mich …** you have the choice **maßlos** *[measureless]*, **tierisch darüber** *[animallike about that]*, **schwarz** *[black]* or **bis zum Gehtnichtmehr** *[until the goes-no-more]*.

You may wonder, where 'ere '80' came from – well it simply refers to those times, when 80 km/h was the absolute speedlimit!

Ich bin auf (hundert-)achtzig/80!
I'm going to explode! *[I am on (1)80]*

Das fängt ja gut an?!
That's a great start? *[that starts just good]*

Freaking out!

Ich krieg 'n Anfall/Rappel!
It's enough to make me throw a fit!
[I get a fit]

Ich krieg zu viel!
I'll freak out! *[I get too much]*

Ich raste/flipp gleich aus!
I'm about to flip!/freak out!
[I disgauge/flip any minute]

Dann war sie nich' mehr zu halten!
There was no holding her back!
[then she was not to hold any more]

Dann is' ihr die Sicherung durchgebrannt!
She just exploded!
[then the fuse has blown on her]

Dann sind ihr die Pferde durchgegangen!
She just lost it!
[then the horses have bolted on her]

Dann klinkte sie einfach aus!
She just lost it! *[then she simply bolted]*

Dann setzte es einfach aus bei ihr!
She just lost it!
[then it simply interrupted in her]

Dann is' sie total ausgetickt/ausgerastet!
She totally freaked out!/blew her top!

Furious! Enough!

Sie springt gleich im Quadrat!
She'll go ballistic!
[she jumps in a square any minute]

You have the choice of other shapes like **Drei-eck** *[triangle]* and **Sechseck** *[hexagon]*. Here you can also use **Riesenstunk** *[giant stink]* and **Riesentrara** *[giant hooha]*:

Terz has multiple meanings: It can be used to refer to the musical third, the tierce in fencing or the third time of the hourly prayer (at 9 am). However, in colloquial language it means 'clamour'. Where this colloquial meaning originates from remains unknown.

Sie machte 'n Riesenterz!
She made a big scene!
[she made a giant clamour]

Sie probt gleich den Aufstand!
She'll make a scene!
[she rehearses the rebellion any minute]

Can't take it!

Some people can just bring your blood to the boil and drive you up the wall:

Der bringt mich ganz schön in Rage!
He really makes me see red!
[he pretty much brings me in rage]

Der bringt mich zur Weißglut/Raserei!
He makes my blood boil!
[he brings me to white embers/frenzy]

Der bringt mich ganz schön auf die Palme!
He drives me up the wall!
[he brings me pretty much on the palm tree]

Die Type hab ich echt gefressen.
I've had it with that guy.
[I have really devoured that (odd) bloke]

Den kann ich einfach nich' ab!
I can't stand him! *[I simply cannot (have) him]*

Instead of **abkönnen** you can use **riechen können** *[can smell]* or **ausstehen können** *[can stand]*.

Crushed!

Er hat mich total zusammengeschissen.
He totally demolished me!
[he has totally shit me together]

Instead of **zusammengeschissen** you may hear **fertig gemacht** *[finished me off]*, **angeschissen** *[shit on]*, **angepfiffen** *[whistled on]*, **angemacht** *[offended]*, **angepisst** *[pissed on]*, **abgekanzelt** *[bawled out]*, **angepflaumt** *[pruned on]*, **angeblafft** *[barked at]*, **zur Sau gemacht** *[turned into a sow]*, **zur Schnecke gemacht** *[turned into a snail]*, **runter gemacht** *[put me down]*, **runtergeputzt** *[washed down]*, **platt gemacht** *[flattened]*, **alle gemacht** *[finished off]* or **in die Pfanne gehauen** *[hit in the pan]*.

In a different context, anmachen *also means 'to come on to someone'.*

Ich hab mir 'n Anschiss eingefangen!
I got quite a bollocking!
[I have caught myself a bollocking]
Er hat mir die Hölle heiß gemacht!

He gave me a piece of his mind!
[he has made hell hot for me]

Enough!

Das halten keine zehn Pferde aus!
No-one can take this much!
[no ten horses endure that]

Das hälst du doch im Kopf nich' aus!
It's just unbearable!
[you just (do) not endure that in the head]

Ich kann's nich' mehr haben/ab!
I can't bear it any more!
[I can have/stand it no more]

Es steht mir bis hier!
I've had it up to here!
[it stands until here in me]

This one will always be accompanied by a gesture showing the height to be above your head or under your chin.

Ich hab's satt!
I'm fed up! *[I have it (=the stomach) full]*

Da hört doch alles auf!
Enough is enough! *[all just stops there]*

Jetzt is' das Maß voll!
That's going too far! *[the measure is full now]*

Hör auf mit dem Scheiß!
Cut the crap!
Jetzt isses langsam gut!

That's enough now! *[it is slowly good now]*

Jetzt wird's mir wirklich zu bunt.
That's it, I've had it!
[it really becomes too coloured for me now]

Das schlägt dem Fass doch den Boden aus!
That's the last straw!
[that just knocks the bottom out of the barrel]

Ich hab die Nase/Schnauze voll!
I have absolutely had it now!
[I have the nose/snout full]

Ich hab die Faxen dicke!
It's not funny any more!
[I have the wisecracks thick]

Jetzt is' Feierabend!
Enough is enough! *[now is party evening]*

Jetzt is' Schicht (im Schacht)!
That's it now! *[it's shift (in the shaft) now]*

Jetzt is' Sense!
Cut it out now! *[it's scythe now]*

Schluss mit lustig!
That's it now! *[end with funny]*

Aus die Maus!
It's over! *[out the mouse]*

Feierabend *is the German word for 'end of work' or 'closing time'. Similarly* Schicht *marks the end of a work shift, while* Sense *refers to cutting short a procedure or argument with a scythe!*

Mind your own business!

Das geht dich (gar) nix an!
It's none of your bloody business!
[*that concerns you nothing (at all)*]

Instead of **gar nix** [*nothing at all*] the more descriptive idioms **'n Scheißdreck** [*a shit dirt*], **'n feuchten Scheißdreck** [*a moist shit dirt*] or **'n feuchten Kehricht** [*a moist sweepings*] can be used as well.

Kümmer dich um deinen (eigenen) Kram!
Mind your own business!
[*look after your (own) stuff*]

Überall muss sie ihre Nase reinstecken!
She's always sticking her nose into other people's business!
[*she must stick her nose into everywhere*]

Get Lost! Or Else …

You can't stand the sight of a person any longer and just want him to get going before you can't control yourself any more:

Verpiss dich!	*[piss off yourself]*	Piss off!
Zieh Leine!	*[pull rope]*	Get lost!
Hau ab!	*[cut down/away]*	Push off!
Verdufte!	*[scent off]*	Bugger off!
Verschwinde!	*[disappear]*	Buzz off!
Schleich dich!	*[scat yourself]*	Get going!
Verzieh dich!	*[scram yourself]*	Sod off!

Zieh Leine probably refers to pulling the rope back onto the ship, and therefore be ready to cast off.

A number of terms starting with **Mach …** *[make]* can be completed with **'ne Fliege** *[a fly]*, **'n Abflug** *[a fly off]*, **die Biege** *[the curve]*, **dich vom Acker** *[yourself of the field/ acre]*, **dich ausm Staub** *[yourself out of the dust]* and **'nen Abgang** *[a step down]*.

You can add Alte(r) [old woman/-man] to the end of these phrases. By the way, you can use Alte(r) if the person is either old or young!

Scher dich zum Teufel/Kuckuck/Henker!
Go to hell!
[shove yourself off to the devil/cuckoo/hangman]

Lass dich hier nie wieder blicken!
Don't ever show your face here again!
[let yourself never be seen again here]

Geh mir aus den Augen!
Get out of my sight!
[go out of my eyes]

Get Lost! Or Else …

Ich mach dir gleich Feuer unterm Hintern!
I'll light a fire under your arse!

Ich werd dir gleich Dampf machen!
I'll make you get a move on!
[I will make steam for you any minute]

Du wirst mich noch kennen lernen!
I'll teach you a thing or two!
[you will get to know me eventually]

Dir wird das Lachen noch vergehen!
You won't be laughing much longer!
[your laughter will wear eventually]

Blasen is short für den Marsch blasen – literally to 'play a march', which is used in the military for commanding people around, right?

Dir werd ich gleich was blasen/husten!
I'll sort you out in a moment!
[I will blow/cough you something any minute]

Na, dir werd ich auf die Sprünge helfen!
I'll show you what's what!
[well, I will help you on the jumps]

Husten is used to express your disdain; the same as spitting someone's face.

Wenn ich den in die Finger/Hände bekomme!
Wait until I get my hands on him!
[when I get him in my fingers/hands]

Den knöpf ich mir mal vor!
I'll sort him out.
[I will (pull) him (in by) his buttons once]

I'll smack you

Gleich setzt es was!
You're gonna get it!

Instead of **was** you can also specify, what awaits the person: **Schläge** *[beatings]* or **'ne Tracht Prügel** *[a good hiding].*

Tracht is an old-fashioned expression for a portion [of food].

Du kannst gleich was erleben!
You're in for it!
[any minute, you can experience something]

Instead of **was** you can use **dein blaues Wunder** *[your blue wonder]* which refers to being black and blue afterwards.

Ich werd dich grün und blau schlagen.
I'll beat you till you're black and blue.
[I will beat you green and blue]

Ich polier dir gleich die (Scheiß-)Fresse!
You're looking for a knuckle sandwich!
[any minute, I polish your (shit) trap]

When dyeing with indigo, the cloth is first green and only turns blue after oxidisation. To get more oxygen into the cloth, it was beaten with sticks, thereby speeding up the process of turning blue.

Instead of **die (Scheiß-)Fresse** you can also say **die Visage** *[mug]*, **die Schnauze** *[snout]*, **die elende Schnauze** *[miserable snout]* or **das Maul** *[muzzle].*

Gleich gibt's eins auf die Fresse!
You're looking for a smack in the mouth!
[any minute, there comes one on the trap]

Get Lost! Or Else …

Gleich bekommst du einen in die Fresse!
I'll bash your face!
[*any minute, you get one on the trap*]

Dez may also be spelled Deez or Dätz!

After **eins/einen** these sentences can end with **aufn Dez** [*on the head*], which is a North German variation of the French 'tête', **auf die Mütze** [*on the beanie*], **auf die Rübe** [*on the turnip*], **auf die Birne** [*on the pear*], **aufn Deckel** [*on the lid*], **aufs Dach** [*on the roof*], which are all familiar expressions for 'head' again, and **auf die Nase** [*on the nose*], **vorn Bug** [*on the ship's bow*] or **aufn Latz** [*on the bib*].

Ich zieh/brat dir gleich eins über!
I'll whack you!
[*I pull/bake one over you any minute*]

Jetzt biste fällig/dran!
You're in trouble now!
[*now you are due / its's your turn*]

Ich knall dir gleich eine!
I'll give it to you in a moment!
[I bang you one any minute]

Instead of **knallen** you can use **scheuern** [to scrub], **kleben** [to glue], **pfeffern** [to pepper], **ballern** [to bang], **langen** [to reach], **wischen** [to wipe] or **verpassen** [to bawl out].

Ich mach dich fertig/alle/kalt!
I'll do you (like a dinner)!
[I make you finished/empty/cold]

Ich werd dich (windel-)weich prügeln!
I'll beat the fuck out of you!
[I will batter you (nappy-)soft]

Ich werd dich zu Mus/Brei schlagen!
I'll beat you to a pulp!

Ich mach Kleinholz/Hackfleisch aus dir!
I'll make mincemeat out of you!
[I will make firewood/mincemeat of you]

Ich werd dich mal ordentlich in die Mangel nehmen!
I'll beat the living daylights out of you!
[I will properly take you in the rotary iron once]

Also usable: **kloppen** [to knock], **vermöbeln** [to pound (with a piece of furniture)], **versohlen** [to spank (with a shoe sole)], **verdreschen** [to thresh] or **zusammenstauchen** [to compress].

Pissing Your Pants?

Scared and close to pissing your pants? This is also known in German:

Der hat die Hosen gestrichen voll!
He's scared shitless! *[he has his pants level full]*

Ich hab 'ne Scheißangst.
I'm scared shitless. *[I have a shit fear]*

Ihm is' das Herz in die Hose gerutscht.
His heart leapt into his throat!
[his heart has slided into his pants]

Da is' mir der Arsch auf Grundeis gegangen.
I pissed my pants.
[then my arse has gone to the ground ice]

Ich hab ganz schön Muffe/Bammel!
I was shitting my pants!
[I pretty much have jitters]

Muffe is the technical term for the end piece of a pipe (known as sleeve). In this idiom an analogy is drawn to the anus and the fact that it contracts when the person experiences pain, anxiety or excitement.

Wimp! Coward!

These are called **Hosenscheißer(in)** *[pants shitter]*, **Schisser(in)** *[shitter]*, **Hosenpisser(in)** *[pants pisser]* or **Hosenpupser(in)** *[pants pooper]* which are best translated as 'chicken'. Then you have **Angsthase** *[fear hare = scaredy cat]*, **Jammerlappen** *[cry cloth = cry baby]*, **Weichei** *[soft egg = wimp]*, **Schwächling** *[weak-*

ling] and **Lusche** *[bitch (dog) = wimpy man].* There is also the **Waschlappen** *[flannel],* **Schlaffi** *[limpy]* and **Schlappschwanz** *[saggy tail = softcock].* In order to talk about cowards, you need: **Memme** *[cissy],* **Feigling** *[coward],* **Duckmäuser(in)** *[ducker = moral coward],* **Drückeberger(in)** *[shirker],* **feige Sau** *[cowardly sow]* or **feiger Hund** *[cowardly dog],* which you may call a 'bloody coward' in English. You also have the **Verlierer(in)** *[loser]* or just the English word **Loser(in)*.**

Among a number of colloquial meanings, Lusche *is also a term to describe the cards in a card game which have no value when tallied at the end of the game.*

Jetzt mach dir nich' ins Hemd!
Don't be scared!
[piss yourself not in the shirt now]

The next are used for party-poopers and all those who tend to spoil the fun:

Jetzt nich' den Schwanz einziehen!
Now don't pull out on me!
[don't pull the tail in now]

Jetzt sei kein Frosch!
Come on pull yourself together!
[be no frog / game spoiler now]

Er ist ein echter Spielverderber!
He's a real bad sport!
[he is a real game spoiler]

Apart from **Spielverderber(in)** there is also **Spaßverderber(in)** *[fun spoiler = killjoy].*

Arseholes, Bitches, Idiots & Others

This is the chapter where you'll find all the fancy negative expressions for both sexes:

Arsehole! Arse!

To voice your anger about any male person, combinations with 'arse' are the key to abusing them in German:

Du blödes Arschloch![1]   **(Du) Arsch![1]**
You stupid arsehole!   (You) arse!

*Verdammt [damned]
and verflucht [cursed]
are used in front of
almost any swearword
to make it even stron-
ger!*

Dieses verdammte/verfluchte Arschloch![1]
This goddamned arsehole!

Was für 'n Arschgesicht!
What an arsehole! *[what an arse face]*

Instead you can use **'n Arsch mit Ohren** *[an arse with ears]* or **'n Riesenarschloch** *[giant arsehole]*.

Die Arschgeige kann mich mal!
That arsehole can get stuffed!
[the arse violin can (have) me once]

Another one involving the 'arse' is **Affenarsch** *[monkey arse]* or a rather soft version is **Arschkeks** *[arse cookie]*. You can also just say **Affe** *[monkey]*.

You can put these combinations into all of the above sentences instead of the arse terms: **Mistkerl**[1] *[manure bloke]*, **Scheißkerl**[1] *[shit bloke]*, **Drecksack**[1] *[dirt sack]*, **Saftsack** *[juice sack]*, **Dreckskerl**[1] *[dirt bloke]*, **Kotzbrocken**[1] *[puke chunk]*, **Stück Scheiße**[1] *[piece of shit]*. This also what you'd say about someone who treats others like a piece of shit:

Der hat mich wie den letzten Dreck behandelt.
He treated me like shit.
[he has treated me like the last dirt]

Instead of **wie den letzten Dreck** you can also use **wie Luft** *[like air]*, **wie 'n Hund** *[like a dog]*, **wie 'n Stück Dreck** *[like a piece of dirt]* or **wie 'n Stück Vieh** *[like a piece of cattle]*.

A **Schuft** is a 'scoundrel' and the following are used for that as well: **Kanake**[1] *[wog]*, **Ganove** *[crook]*, **Halunke** *[rascal]*, **Gauner** *[rogue]*, **Lump** *[rook]*, **Schurke** *[knave]*, **Bandit** *[bandit]* or the French word **Kanaille.**

Was für 'n Abschaum![1]
What a scum(bag)!

Nich' der Fatzke/Futzi/Heini or **die Type ?!**
Not that (odd) bloke?

Du bist echt das Letzte/Allerletzte!
You're really the worst piece of shit!
[you are really the last/very last]

You need to alter your tone of voice when saying 'Not that (odd) bloke' as if it meant 'arsehole'.

Pig! Rat!

Another set of curses for male individuals makes use of 'pigs': **(dumme) Sau**[1] *[(dumb) sow]*, **(mieses) Schwein**[1] *[(lousy) pig]*, **Sauhund**[1] *[sow dog]*, **Saukerl**[1] *[sow bloke]*, **Drecksau**[1] *[dirt sow]* and **Dreckschwein**[1] *[dirt pig]*. Then **Schweinehund**[1] *[pig dog]*, which implies some type of meanness, **Schweinebacke** *[pig cheek]*, which generally addresses a double crossing bastard and **Schweinepriester** *[pig priest]*, if the bloke has particularly filthy morals, or is just a real hypocrite. However, this combination is synonymous for 'poor bugger': **Arme Sau!** *[poor sow]*.

Pigheaded people are not at all referred to with 'piggy connotations': **Dickkopf** *[thick head]*, **Dickschädel** *[thick skull]*, **Sturkopf** *[stubborn head]* or **Betonkopf** *[concrete head]*.

The rat, or variations thereof are also used as insults for men: **Ratte** *[rat]*, **Kanalratte** *[canal rat]*, **Beutelratte** *[marsupial rat]* or **Bisamratte** *[muskrat]*.

Cocksucker!

Similarly, Wichserin can be used to describe females (meaning 'bitch').

Curses for men with sexual connotations are **Wichser**[1] *[wanker/jerk]* or **Flachwichser**[1] *[flat wanker/jerk]* if you want to insinuate that he doesn't get too far with his sperm. Very funny is also **Schmalspurwichser**[1] *[narrow gauge wanker]*, which I leave to your imagination to visualise.

More insults include **Hurensohn**[1] *[whore's son]*, **Hurenbock**[1] *[whore's buck]*, **Bastard** *[bastard]*, **Missgeburt**[1] *[miscarriage]* or **Zuhälter** *[pimp]*. And last but not least there are **Schwanzgesicht**[1] *[tail face]* and **Schwanzlutscher**[1] *[tail licker]*, the latter being the German equivalent for 'cocksucker'.

Despite the fact that the big German cities take an increasingly liberal stand towards the gay community, there are still swear words for the perpetual homophobic. Gay men are called **Schwuchtel**[1] *[faggot]*, **Tucke**[1] *[poofter]* or **Tunte**[1] *[fairy]*. Even worse is **schwule Sau**[1] *[gay pig]*. Then there are zillions of variations on **Arschficker**[1] *[arse fucker]*, which I prefer to name in detail.

Not gay is a **Transe**[1] *[transvestite]*, but it's nevertheless used as a swear word for gay men with a feminine touch. There is a rather cute way to express, that someone is homosexual:

Der is' vom anderen Ufer!
He bats for the other side!
[he is from the other shore]

Idiot!

This is probably the curse with the most variety. First you can start abusing the dimwit:
Dummkopf *[dumb head]*, **Doofkopf** *[imbecile head]*, **Blödkopf** *[daft head]*, **Knallkopf** *[bang head]*, **Hohlkopf** *[hollow head]*, **Schwachkopf** *[weak head]* or **Döskopf** *[doze head]*.

Arseholes, Bitches, Idiots & Others

Der is' doch dümmer als die Polizei erlaubt!
He's so stupid, he shouldn't even be walking the streets!
[he is just dumber than allowed by the police]

Der is' doch dämlich wie Schifferscheiße!
He's thick as shit!
[he is just goony like skipper shit]

For men's stupidity: **verdammter Idiot** *[damned idiot]*, **Doofmann** *[imbecile man]*, **Blödmann** *[daft man]*, **Blödian** *[daft person]*, **Depp** *[twit]*, **Knalltüte** *[bang bag]*. The simple-minded are: **Einfaltspinsel** *[simpleton]*, **Dumpfbacke** *[dull cheek]*, **Gollo** *[dope]*, **trübe Tasse** *[dim cup]* and those who are crazy: **Spinner** *[spinner = nutcase]*.

Possbilities to express that someone is mad, were introduced in the chapter 'Crazy! Driving Me Nuts'.

Some people are described as 'slow on the uptake', which is **begriffsstutzig** *[slow-witted]* or **schwer von Kapee** *[difficult concerning comprehension]*. To avoid addressing the person directly you just sigh and mumble:

Wenn Dummheit wehtäte ...
[if dumbness would hurt]

The clumsy: **(Ober-/Voll-)Trottel** *[(top/full) moron]*, **Trollo** *[little moron]*, **Trampel** *[lump]*, **Dussel** *[duffer]*, **Armleuchter** *[candelabra = bonehead]*, **Schussel** *[fidget]*, **Tölpel** *[dolt]*, **Tollpatsch** *[clumsy person]*, **Pappnase** *[cardboard nose]* as reference to a clown's nose, **Hanswurst** *[Hans sausage]* or **Flasche** *[bottle]*.

A Hanswurst was a comical figure in the German theater of the 18th century.

Was für unterbelichteter Penner!
What a stupid bastard!
[what an underexposed bum]

If you pity an idiot, it's probably ein armer Willi *[a poor Willy] or* ein armer Tropf *[a poor drip].*

Der hat doch 'n beschränkten Horizont!
He's got a limited horizon!

Terms from the animal world include **Spatzenhirn** [sparrow brain], **Esel** [donkey], **Rindvieh** [cattle animal], **(Horn-)Ochse** [(horn) ox], **Mondkalb** [moon calf] or **Schaf** [sheep].

Bitch!

For women you combine dumbness with an animal: **dumme Kuh** [dumb cow]. Instead of **Kuh** you can insert **Ziege/Zicke** [goat], **Gans** [goose], **Pute** [female turkey] or **Huhn** [chicken]. Also nice are **Suppenhuhn** [soup chicken] and **Sumpfhuhn** [swamp chicken].

To all of these you can add blöde(s) *[daft] or even* doofe(s) *[imbecile] instead of* dumme *[dumb].*

Die is' doch dumm wie Bohnenstroh!
She's thick as shit!
[she is just dumb like bean straw]

You can also simply use derogative equivalents for 'women' with an annoyed tone of voice: **blöde Tussi**[1], **blöde Tusnelda**[1] or **blöde Trulla**[1]. All literally mean 'daft wench'! Along similar lines is **Tröte,** which is really Low German for 'dumb woman'. **Schickse** is a Yiddish word for 'Christian slut', which is generally used the same as the above.

Arseholes, Bitches, Idiots & Others

Vergiss die Tante!
Forget about that bitch! *[forget the aunt]*

Dummes Weibstück![1]
Stupid bitch! *[dumb piece of woman]*

Very common is also the use of **Schnalle** *[dog's cunt; in hunter's terms]*, although most people are not even familiar any more with its literal meaning. Then there is also **(dumme) Schnepfe[1]** *[(dumb) snipe]*.

If you want to use more rough stuff, you'll have to go into sexual insinuations, which boil down to calling her a 'whore' in many ways: **Schlampe[1]** *[bitch]* and even more are **(billiges) Flittchen[1]** *[(cheap) slut]*, **Nutte[1]** *[hooker]*, **Hure[1]** *[whore]*, or **Fotze[1]** *[cunt]*.

Popular adjectives to make the statement even stronger are blöde *[daft],* alte *[old] or* dreckige *[dirty].*

The nasty ones get accused of being a **Luder** *[minx]*, **Biest** *[beast]*, **Zimtzicke** *[cinnamon goat]*, **Schlange** *[snake]*, **falsche Schlange[1]** *[deceiving snake]* or very bad as **hinterfotzige Kuh[1]** *[cow with a back(stabbing) cunt]* – really meaning 'backstabbing cow'.

Zimt *is an old term for things considered to be nonsense or unworthy, but it also means 'cinnamon'.*

Sie is' 'ne echte Kratzbürste!
She's a real bitch! *[real scratch brush]*

Arse-kisser

Those who suck up to others are **Schleimer(in)** *[slimer]*, **Speichellecker(in)** *[saliva licker]* or even worse **Schleimscheißer(in)** *[slime shitter]*, **Arschkriecher(in)[1]** *[arse crawler]*.

Der hat sich wieder bei ihr eingeschleimt.
He's been sucking up to her again.
[he slimed himself in her again]

Der kriecht echt jedem in den Arsch.
He sucks up to everyone.
[he really crawls everyone into the arse]

The fat and skinny

You can call him **Fettarsch**[1] *[fat arse]*, **Fettsack**[1] *[fat sack]*, **Fettsau**[1] *[fat sow]*, **Fettwanst**[1] *[fat paunch]*, **fette Tonne**[1] *[fat barrel]*, **Fettkloß**[1] *[fat dumpling]*; **Fettfleck**[1] *[fat stain]* also works for her.

You can also combine certain animals with **dick** *[big/fat]* or **fett** *[fat]* and have a popular curse for a fat person. The male ones are **Fette Sau!**[1] or **Fettes Schwein!**[1] and the females **Fette Kuh!**[1] or **Dicke Ziege!**[1]

Die hat 'n Arsch wie 'n Brauereipferd.[1]
She's got a huge arse!
[she has an arse like a brewery horse]

These are mostly used to tease rather than call the person names.

Much more imaginative are names for skinny men: **Spargeltarzan** [asparagus Tarzan] or **(langer) Lulatsch** [long skinny person], **Hänfling** [bony person, but also a little bird]. For both genders you can use **Gerippe** [skeleton], **Klappergestell** [clack rack] and then there's **Bohnenstange** [beanpole] for women.

The short and young

Short men or little boys are called **Knilch** [chap], **Knirps** [chit], **Zwerg** [dwarf], **Schlumpf** [smurf], **halbes Hemd** [half shirt] or **Halbaffe** [half monkey] Both girls and boys can be named **Kurze(r)** [shorty], **Pimpf** [moppet], **Wicht** [gnome], **Winzling** [tiny thing], **Hosenscheißer(in)** [pants shitter] or **halbe Portion** [half portion].

Boys who look too young can be named **Bubi** [little boy] or **Milchbubi** [little milk boy]. If they are too dependent on their mother, it's a **Muttersöhnchen** [mummy's little son].

Grünschnabel [green beak] and **Rotznase** [snot nose] are those who're still 'wet behind the ears':

Der is' noch feucht hinter den Ohren.
He's so juvenile!

Little boys who behave like smartarses can be addressed like this: **Na, du Neunmalklug!** [well, you nine times smart] or ... **Dreikäsehoch!** [three cheeses high].

Naughty kids are **Bengel** *[rascal]*, **Flegel** *[cub]*, **Blag** *[brat]*, **Rabauke** *[troublemaker]*, **Schlawiner** *[wangler]*, **Satansbraten** *[satan's roast]*, **Strolch** *[rascal]*, **Schlingel** *[cheat]*, **Spitzbube** *[scallywag]*, **Lausbube** *[little louse boy]*, **(ausgekochtes) Schlitzohr** *[(boiled out) slit ear]* which is also a 'cheat' or **Lümmel** *[mischief]*. If these boys (or girls) have been teasing you: **Na warte, du kleine Kröte!** *[well wait, you little toad]*.

In former times, crooks used to be punished by having their ears slit.

Kids who always come home dirty or make a mess: **Dreckspatz** *[dirty sparrow]*, **Schmierfink** *[smear finch]* or **Ferkel** *[piglet]*. With a sigh parents complain about their brat:

Er hat's faustdick hinter den Ohren.
He's a crafty one.
[he has it fist thick behind the ears]

The nasty

Widerling, Fiesling, Ekel are all 'disgusting men' or 'creeps'. If the bloke is lusting after you in an unpleasant stalking manner, you call him **Geiler Bock!**[1] *[horny buck]* or **Spanner** *[voyeur]*.

Old ladies, who keep nagging: **Spinatwachtel** *[spinach quail:* a funny looking old lady), **Gewitterziege** *[thunderstorm goat]*, **Tucke** *[nasty woman; but also: poofter]*, **Schabracke** *[horse]*, **Giftspritze** *[old poison syringe]*, **Xanthippe** *[gaunt woman]*, **Schreckschraube** *[fright screw]* or **Drachen** *[old dragon]*.

You may want to add alte(r) *[old] in front of any of these.*

Die hat Haare aufn Zähnen!
She's a nasty old bitch!
[she has hair on the teeth]

Similarly old nagging men are called: **Giftzwerg** *[poison dwarf]*, at least when they are not tall. Another nice one is **Korinthenkacker(in)** *[raisin cacker]* which is either some 'whinging old bastard' or a 'stingy bastard'. Those rule abiding people can be abused as **Spießer(in)** *[bourgeois]*.

Mit dem/ihr is' nich' gut Kirschen essen!
It's best not to tangle with him/her.
[you can't eat cherries well with him/her]

A grumpy man of any age is called **Stinkstiefel** *[stink boot]* or **Stinktier** *[stink animal; also: skunk]*. An old man is an **alter Knacker** *[old geezer]*.

Cash & Work

Lots of hard work may result in lots of spending money. These are all idiomatic terms for cash: **Asche** *[ashes]*, **Eier** *[eggs]*, **Flocken** *[flakes]*, **Flöhe** *[fleas]*, **Kies** *[pebbles]*, **Knete** *[dough]*, **Kohle** *[coal]*, **Kröten** *[toads]*, **Mäuse** *[mice]*, **Moneten** *[money]*, **Moos** *[moss]*, **Möpse** *[pugs]*, **Mücken** *[mosquitos]*, **Ocken** *[?; unclear origin]*, **Piepen** *[birdies]*, referring to the eagle on the old German Mark coins, **Penunsen** *[Polish word for money]*, **Schotter** *[gravel]* or **Zaster** *[metal]*. If there's lots of it you can create expressions like these: '**n Batzen Kohle** *[a batch of coal]*, '**n Haufen Asche** *[a heap of ash]* or '**ne Stange Geld** *[a rod of money]*.

If you have a lot of money, you've probably been busy with **Geld scheffeln** *[to shovel money]*, which is an idiom for 'to work'.

Kohle was used as currency after the Second World War. It's easy to understand where the terms Geld scheffeln *or* Asche *came from then.*

There are numerous other idiomatic terms for specific monetary items: Riesen *[giants] are banknotes worth 1.000,* Blaue *[blue ones] used to be those worth 100 in times of the Deutsche Mark,* Fuffi *[one of fifty] is a 50 and a counterfeited banknote is called* Blüte *[bloom].*

Well off

Der verdient sich 'ne goldene Nase.
He earns a pretty penny.
[he earns himself a golden nose]

Der macht voll den Reibach.
He makes a killing. *[he fully makes the interest]*

Die leben in Saus und Braus.
They live like lords.
[they live in whistle (of the wind) and break (of the surf)]

Der hat Geld wie Heu.
He's got money to burn.
[he has money like hay]

Die schwimmen in Geld.
They're rolling in money.
[they swim in money]
They are **wohlhabend** *[well-off]*, **vermögend**

[with assets], **reich** [rich], **steinreich** [stone rich], **unanständig reich** [indecently rich] and **millionenschwer** [millions heavy]. An unpleasant trait of the rich is often to be **knauserig, knickerig** or **geizig** [all: stingy].

Der hat 'n Haufen Asche abgestaubt.

He cleaned up.

[he has dusted off a heap of money]

'Der hat 'n Haufen Asche abgestaubt.' *originally refers to inheritances.*

Instead of **abgestaubt** you can use **abgeräumt** [cleared off], **abgesahnt** [creamed off], **angehäuft** [heaped up], **eingesackt** [bagged] and **eingestrichen** [confiscated].

Broke

Ich bin blank.

I'm broke. [I am bare]

Ich bin total abgebrannt.

I'm totally broke. [I am totally burned down]

Ich bin chronisch pleite.

I'm always broke.

[I am chronically bankrupt]

Ich hab gerade wenig Kohle.

I'm a bit strapped for cash at the moment.

[I currently have little coal]

Bei mir herrscht Ebbe (im Geldbeutel).

I'm broke. [there reigns low tide (in my purse)]

Ich bin was knapp/schwach bei Kasse.
I'm short of cash.
[I am slightly tight/weak in the cash box]

Ich muss den Gürtel enger schnallen.
I have to tighten my belt.

Ich steh dick in der Kreide.
I'm burdened with loans.
[I stand thick in chalk]

Es fehlt an allen Ecken und Enden.
I'm doing poorly.
[it lacks at all corners and ends]

Mir fehlt's hinten und vorne.
I'm struggling.
[I lack it back and front]

Helping hand and resignation

If someone points out that you could borrow
a little bit of money or sell something:

Ich würd dir gern aus der Patsche helfen.
I'd like to help you out.
[I would like to help you out of the mud]

Instead of **Patsche** you can also use **Klemme**
[clamp], **Tinte** *[ink]* and **Bredouille** *[tight spot]*.

Ich kann dir was pumpen.
I can lend you some. *[I can pump you some]*

Das kannste für lau haben.
You can have it for free.

Du kannst ja deine CDs* verscherbeln.
You can flog off your CDs.

Other idiomatic words for selling stuff are **verschachern** [to barter away], **verticken** [to vend], **verhökern** [to hawk] and **verschleudern** [to monger].

Das macht den Kohl auch nich' fett.
That won't help either.
[that makes the cabbage not fat either]

Das is' auch nur 'n Tropfen aufn heißen Stein.
That's just a drop in the ocean.
[that is only a drop on the hot stone too]

So komm ich nie auf 'n grünen Zweig.
I'll never get on top again.
[that way, I never come onto a green twig]

Ich krieg kein Bein auf die Erde.
I just can't get on top of things.
[I get no leg on the ground]

Expensive

Der Lappen geht ganz schön ins Geld.
A driver's licence costs a pretty penny.
[the cloth goes pretty much into the money]

Lappen *is generally used to refer to a small (old) piece of cloth, but may also be used to denote a driver's licence or a banknote.*

Dafür kann ich nich' auch noch blechen.
I can't fork out more money for that!

Instead of **blechen** you can use **Kohle hinblättern** *[to leaf down coal = to put down money]*. To scrape together some money is called **Kohle berappen** *[to rack up coal]* or **Knete zusammenkratzen** *[to scrape together dough]*.

Blech *is another equivalent for money in the old German Rotwelsch language. Therefore blechen means 'to pay'.*

Das hat 'n großes Loch in die Kasse gerissen.
That put a big hole in my pocket.
[that has ripped a big hole in the cash box]

Da kann man gleich sein Geld zum Fenster rauswerfen.
I might as well throw my money away.
[one can immediately throw one's money out the window then]

Die ziehen einem echt das Geld aus der Tasche.
That's daylight robbery.
[they really pull the money out of one's pocket]

Ich hab tief in die Kasse greifen müssen.
I had to dig deep.
[I have had to reach deep into the cash box]

Croesus was the last king of Lydia (reigned c. 560–546), and was renowned for his great wealth.

Bin ich Krösus?
You think, I'm made of money? *[am I Croesus]*

Es gibt keine Extrawürste.
There'll be no special treatment.
[there are no extra sausages]

If the money is all spent, it's **alles verbraten** *[all frittered away]*, **verbuttert** *[churned]*, **verprasst** *[sizzled away]*, **verschwendet** *[wasted]*, **verpulvert** *[pulverised]*, **vergeudet** *[misspent]*, **verjubelt** *[cheered away]* or if it was gambled: **verspielt** *[played away]*, **verwettet** *[bet away]* and **verzockt** *[Yiddish for gambled]*.

Work

Work is a topic people will always whinge about. For 'to work very hard' you use **sich** *[oneself]* with **abarbeiten** *[to work hard]*, **abrackern** *[to drudge]*, **abplagen** *[to plod]*, **abquälen** *[to torment]*, **abmühen** *[to trouble]*, **abschinden** *[to grind]*, **abstrampeln** *[to struggle]* and **krumm arbeiten** *[to work until bent]*.

Ich schufte mich zu Tode.
I'm slaving away. *[I toil myself to death]*

Ich schufte wie 'n Pferd.
I'm working my guts out.
[I toil like a horse]

Ich arbeite mir die Finger wund.
I'm working my fingers to the bone.
[I work my fingers wounded]

Ich arbeite mich dumm und dusslig.
I've worked my arse off.
[I work myself dumb and numb]

Other idiomatic terms for 'to work' are **ma-lochen** *[to work hard]*, **schaffen** *[to labour]*, **ölen** *[to oil]*, **rödeln** *[to peg]*, **ackern** *[to plow]*, **ochsen** *[to use the ox on the fields]* and **büffeln** *[to use the buffalo on the fields]*.

Hardship

If you want to speak more globally about the trouble you went through:

Ich hab mir echt 'n (Ast) abgebrochen.
I've been struggling.
[I have really broke myself off a (branch)]

Ich hab mir den Arsch aufgerissen.
I put in so much effort.
[I have ripped my arse open]

'To be on the dole' is called stempeln gehen *[to go stamp]. In former times, it was customary to stamp the papers of a beneficiary on the day of payment, to ensure that they could not receive the funds twice.*

Instead of **den Arsch aufgerissen** you can also give your limbs: **'n Arm ausgerissen** *[ripped out an arm]* or **'n Bein ausgerissen** *[ripped out a leg]*.

A very special type of hardship can be experienced when you have to run around busily in order to get something done: **rumgurken** *[cucumber around]*, **rumgondeln** *[gondola around]*, all mean that you've been on a wild goose chase and couldn't find your destination.

Very similar is **rumeiern** *[egg around]*, but you are shaky while doing it, **rumbrettern** *[board around]* and **rumkurven** *[curve around]* are direction-less drives with a vehicle. **Abklappern** *[clack along]* expresses that you go from door to door in order to get something done, **ablatschen** *[slouch along]* is used for any lengthy walk which wasn't fun.

Partytime! Get Plastered!

For some, the best way to relax after a hard day's work is to either hit the pub, or go to a party with your mates.

Haste Bock einen drauf zu machen?
Fancy a night out?
[have you (got an) urge to make one on it]

Instead of with **einen drauf zu machen** you can complete the sentence like this:

Partytime! Get Plastered!

... auf die Piste/Rolle zu gehen?
[to go on the track/pulley]
... a night out?

... die Stadt unsicher zu machen?
[to make the city unsafe]
...to paint the town red.

If Germans plan to have a night in and their spouses or parents are out, they often say:

Ich hab heut sturmfreie Bude.
I've got the house to myself today.
[I have a storm free booth today]

A drinking spree

If people refer to a drinking spree, they may explicitly state:

Lass uns 'ne Sauftour machen.
Let's go on a drinking spree.
[let us make a booze tour]

Instead of **Sauftour** you can fill in **Kneipentour** *[pub crawl]*, **Kneipenbummel** *[pub stroll]* or **Zechtour** *[quaff tour]*. A tongue-in-cheek expression in the river Rhine area is **Rheintour** *[rhine tour]* – a play on words with **rein,** which means 'into' and illustrates how you keep going into one pub after another. This is something you would enjoy with a good drinking mate of your's, who's called **Saufkumpel** or **Saufkumpan** *[booze mate]*.

Rolle is short for Seilrolle *(pulley) which is equivalent to the old word* Walz(e).
The redundant auf die Walz gehen, *describes the life of handicraftsmen on the road, which often involved patronising the pubs in each town that was visited.*

Interestingly, this is also the origin for the famous Australian song 'Waltzing Matilda', which refers to an Australian style sleeping bag (swag = matilda) 'on the waltz'. This style sleeping bag was used by early German settlers in South Australia.

Partytime! Get Plastered!

Wie wär's mit 'nem Absacker?
How about a nightcap?
[how would it be with a drop off]

References to the chest are made, because that's the height to which you raise the drink for a toast.

Lass uns noch einen zur Brust nehmen.
Let's have another drink.
[let us take another one to the chest]

Instead of **zur Brust nehmen** you can also use **genehmigen** *[to allow]*, **heben** *[to raise]*, **zechen** *[to quaff]*, **picheln** *[to level]*, **löten** *[to solder]* or **zwitschern** *[to chirp]*. To understate things even more **'n Schlückchen trinken** *[to drink a little sip]* or you can imitate the sound of opening a beer by saying **'n Bier zischen** *[to fizz a beer]* or **wegzischen** *[to fizz away]*.

More words for 'drinking alcohol' are: **bechern** *[to beaker]*, **schlürfen** *[to slurp]*, **reinschütten** *[to pour in]* **süffeln** *[to guzzle]*, **reinziehen** *[to pull in]* or **weghauen** *[to knock back]*. With the intention of getting drunk at all cost:

Ich werd mir einen hinter die Binde kippen.
I'll wet my whistle.
[I will throw myself one behind the tie]

Ich werd mich voll laufen lassen.
I'll get drunk. *[I will let myself run full]*

Ich werd mir voll die Kante geben.
I'll give myself a hammering.
[I will fully give myself the edge]

Ich werd dich unter den Tisch saufen.
I'll drink you under the table.

One cultural aspect which is specific to the German language is the 'official' end of using the formal **Sie** to address someone and to begin using each other's first name, or the informal **du.** This is done by one person offering:

Lass uns Brüderschaft trinken!
[let us drink (to) brotherhood]

An important detail to understand correctly, might be **Auf ex!** or in Latin: **Ad fundum!** which both mean 'Bottoms up!'.

The ritual proceeds as follows: You stand opposite each another and raise your glasses.
You then hook your drinking arms around each other, bringing the glass to your mouth and emptying the glass (while your arms remain intertwined) and then finish off by kissing each other either on the mouth, or once on each cheek.
Each person then says their first name, indicating that from then onwards, you are on informal terms.

Partytime! Get Plastered!

A blast

Once you wake up hungover you can comment on your night out:

Wir haben so richtig aufn Putz gehauen.
We really whooped it up.
[we have just really hit on the plaster]

Alternatively you can swap **aufn Putz gehauen** with **auf die Pauke gehauen** *[hit the drums]* or **die Sau rausgelassen** *[let out the sow]*. To vary **richtig** *[right]* you can use **mächtig** *[forceful]* or **anständig** *[decently]*.

Wir haben's so richtig krachen lassen!
We had a real blast!
[we have just really let it blast]

The origin of this idiom is rather complicated: Puppen seems to refer to statues in Berlin's Tiergarten park in the 18th century. To get there from the city was a very long walk. So if you partied so hard that you'd end up there, it had been a long night!

Die Party* ging bis spät in die Puppen!
The party went until late.
[the party went until late in the puppets]

Wir haben gefeiert bis zum Abwinken!
We partied until we dropped.
[we have partied until waving 'enough']

Much more cynical seems the use of **bis zur Vergasung** *[until the gassing]*. It refers to chemistry, where a heated substance reaches its final physical form of gas. Since the gassing of Jews in the Third Reich, this idiom is considered inappropriate.

Da geht der Bär ab.
The place is cracking.
[there goes off the bear]

Instead of **geht der Bär ab** you can use **geht die Post ab** *[runs off the post]*, **tanzt der Bär** *[dances the bear]*, **steppt der Bär** *[tap dances the bear]*, **tobt der Bär** *[rollicks the bear about]*, **is' die Hölle los** *[hell is loose]* or **is' voll was los** *[something is fully loose]*.

Bär refers to the bear as the main attraction on travelling country fairs.

Hier is' immer Remmidemmi!
There's always something happening here.
[here is always rumble/noise]

Es hat echt Fez gemacht!
It was really fun!
[it has really made (the) party]

The origin of Fez is unclear, but it's believed to derive of the French plural for 'parties': fêtes.

Das hat's doch echt gebracht.
That really did it.
[that has just really brought it]

Es war 'ne Bombenstimmung!
It was a blast!
[it was a bomb atmosphere]

Jetzt kommt Schwung/Leben in die Bude!
The fun is only starting now.
[now comes swing/life in the hut]

Then you still have the possibility of the party being a total failure:

Da war echt tote Hose!
It was very boring!
[there were really dead pants]

Das war voll der Flop/Reinfall.
That was such a flop.
[that was fully the flop/downfall]

Es war 'ne (Riesen-)Pleite.
It was a (big) flop.
[it was a (giant) bankruptcy]

Instead of **Pleite** you can use **Bruchlandung** *[crash-landing]*, **Bauchlandung** *[belly-landing]*, **Schiffbruch** *[shipwreck]*, **Fehltritt** *[misstep]*, **Fiasko** *[fiasco]* or **Schlappe** *[floppy one]*.

Jetzt haben wir den Salat!
Now look at the mess!
[now we have the salad]

The well understood result of alcoholic beverage consumption is some tipsy silliness: **gut dabei** *[good at it]*, **angetrunken** *[drunk up]*, **angeheitert** *[cheered up]* **angeschickert** or **schicker** *[guzzled up]*, **angezwitschert** *[chirped up]*, **angesäuselt** *[purred up]*, **beschwipst** *[tipsy]*, **betütert** or **angetüdelt** *[North German for 'tipsy']*, **berauscht** *[intoxicated]*, **bierselig** *[beer blessed]*, **weinselig** *[wine blessed]*, **beduselt** *[woozy]* or **benebelt** *[fogged up]*.

Ich hab wohl 'n Schwips.
I think I'm a bit tipsy.

Plain old 'drunk' would be **betrunken** *[drunk]*, **besoffen** *[boozed]*, **blau** *[blue]*, **breit** *[broad]*, **bedröhnt** *[roared]*, **stramm** *[taut]* or **knülle** *[tight]*. Had one too many?

Sie hat einen in der Krone.
[she has one in the crown/head]
Sie hat schon einen sitzen.
[she has one (monkey) sitting]
Sie hat einen im Tee.
[she has one (rum) in the tea]
Sie hat einen im Kahn.
[she has one in the barge]
Sie hat schon einen intus.
[she has one in already]

When a lot of bullshit is talked, you call it **voll** *[full]*, **dicht** *[tight]* or **zu** *[closed]*. Similarly **abgefüllt** *[filled up]*, **randvoll** *[full to the rim]*, **vollgetankt** *[fully tanked]* and **volltrunken** *[fully drunk]* illustrate the process of filling up. You can go one step further and call it **hackedicht** and **hackezu** meaning 'drunk to the heel'. To describe someone as 'completely tanked', you may say:

Er hat den Kanal voll.
[he has the canal full]
Der is' voll wie 'ne (Strand-)Haubitze.
[he is full like a beach slingshot]

Partytime! Get Plastered!

Der is' voll wie 'ne Natter.
[he is full like an adder]
Der hat ganz schön geladen.
[he has loaded pretty much]
Er hat einen über'n Durst getrunken.
[he has drunk one past his thirst]
Er wohl 'n bisschen zu tief ins Glas geschaut.
[he just looked a bit too deep in the glass]
Der hat schon Schlagseite.
[he is listing already]

The preferred idiom for the kind of drunkenness where you can't walk straight any more is **sturzbetrunken** or **sturzbesoffen,** since **Sturz** means 'fall'. Similarly you can say **stockbetrunken** and **stockbesoffen,** whereby **Stock** means 'stick'.

Even worse is **sternhagelvoll** [star hail full], which describes seeing little blinking stars after passing out. Another favourite is **granatenvoll** [grenade full] or **stritzebesoffen** in the river Rhine region. Other variations are **zugedröhnt** [roared closed] or **zugelötet** [soldered closed]. Ultimately you describe the person as 'far gone':

The word Kater *derives of 'Katarrh', which is the old word for 'runny nose' in conjunction with a headache; both symptoms of a beer-hangover.*

Er is' über'n Jordan.
[he is over the Jordan (river)]
Der is' total hinüber.
[he is totally over it]
Er is' schon jenseits von Gut und Böse.
[he is already beyond good and evil]

Someone who drinks too much is called **Trinker(in)** *[drinker]*, **Säufer(in)** *[boozer]*, **Saufbold** *[booze goblin]*, **Trunkenbold** *[drunk goblin]*, **Zecher** *[boozer]*, **Alki** *[alcoholic]*, with 'birdy' connotations: **Schnapsdrossel** *[liquor thrush]*, **Schluckspecht** *[swallow woodpecker]*.

In very bad competitive cases **Kampftrinker(in)** *[fight drinker]* or **Komatrinker(in)** *[coma drinker]* can be used.

Hungover

Ich hab 'n (ausgewachsenen) Kater.
I've got a bad hangover.
[I have a (full-grown) hangover]

Instead of **Kater** you can also use **Katzenjammer** *[cat brawl]*, **Brummschädel** *[drone skull]* and **dicken Schädel** *[thick skull]*.

Kater *also means 'tomcat'!*

Mir brummt der Schädel.
My head's splitting.
[my skull drones]

The 'skull' can be substituted with **der Kopf** *[head]* and **die Birne** *[pear]*.

Ich hab 'n Filmriss.
I have a blackout. *[I have a film rip]*

Er hat seinen Rausch ausgeschlafen.
He slept it off.
[he has slept off his intoxication]

Puke

During a heavy drinking session, your body may have had it with the intoxicating intake and just chucks it back out. This is called **kotzen** *[to puke]*, **brechen** *[to chuck]*, **erbrechen** *[to heave]*, **göbeln** *[to retch]*, **kübeln** *[to spew in buckets]*, **reihern** *[to spew like a heron]*, **speien** *[to spew]*, **spucken** *[to spit]* or **sich übergeben** *[to throw up]*.

Mir is' schlecht/übel/kotzübel/speiübel!
I feel (as) sick as a dog.
[I am bad/sick/puke sick/spew sick]

Ihm kommt's schon hoch.
He's regurgitating. *[it comes up in him]*

Munch, Devour & Eat

Once you've made some room, you can fill your empty stomach again. The process of eating can idiomatically be described as **futtern** *[to scoff]*, **verputzen** *[to clean up]*, **mampfen** *[to gobble]*, **verdrücken** *[to push in]*, **zwischen die Kiemen schieben/klemmen** *[to shove/wedge between the gills]*, **reinschieben** *[to shove in]*, **einschmeißen** *[to throw in]*, **was einwerfen** *[to throw something in]*, **sich reinhauen** *[to hit in oneself]*, **verspeisen** *[to ingest]*, **sich stärken** *[to strengthen oneself]*, **löffeln** *[to spoon up]*, **vertilgen** *[to exterminate]* and **sich was zu essen krallen** *[to claw something to eat]*. Getting hungry now?

Mir läuft das Wasser im Mund zusammen.
That's making my mouth water.
[the water runs together in my mouth]

If you have nothing to eat and you get increasingly hungry, you say **Ich hab Kohldampf!** or substitute **Kohldampf** with **'n Bärenhunger** *[bear's hunger]*, **'n Mordshunger** *[murderous hunger]*, **'n mordsmäßigen Hunger** *[murderous-like hunger]*, **'n saumäßigen Hunger** *[sow-like hunger]*, **Riesenhunger** *[giant hunger]*, **'n Wahnsinnshunger** *[mad hunger]* or **rasenden Hunger** *[raging hunger]*.

The notion of a craving is **Heißhunger** *[hot hunger]* or simply **Appetit** *[appetite]*.

Kohldampf can be mistaken to literally mean 'cabbage steam', but the expression 'Kohl' really refers to the Rotwelsch words Kohler *and* Dampf, *which both mean 'hunger'!*

Haste was zu beißen da?
[have you (got) something to bite there]
Haste was für zwischen die Kiemen?
[have you (got) something for between the gills]
Both: Got something to eat?

Once you've given someone something to eat, you encourage them to go for it:

Hau rein, Alte(r)!
Dig in, man!

If it's implied that large quantities are devoured, you can vary **essen** *[to eat]* with **fressen** *[to devour]*, **sich vollfressen** *[to devour oneself full]*, **spachteln** *[to putty]*, **den Bauch vollschlagen** *[to hit the belly full]*, **verschlingen** *[to guzzle]*, **fressen wie 'n Scheunendrescher** *[to devour like a barn harvester]*, **sich was reinstopfen** *[to stuff something in oneself]* or **herunterschlingen** *[to gorge down]*.

Wo bunkerst du die Fressalien?
Where do you hide the grub?
[where (do) you bunker the 'devourables']

The more sophisticated way to eat would be: **speisen** *[to ingest]*, **dinieren** *[to dine]* or **tafeln** *[to table]*. When it tastes really great it's **schlemmen** or **schmausen** *[both: to feast]*. More of a nibble is **naschen** *[to snack]*, **knabbern** *[to munch]*, **knuspern** *[to crunch]* and slow munching is called **mümmeln** *[to nosh]*.

Chatting Up & Knocked Back

A German saying claims **Liebe geht durch den Magen** *[love goes through the stomach]*, so food is closely linked to 'being in love'.

Der/die sieht zum Anbeißen aus!
He/she has looks to die for!
[he/she looks to take a bite into]

You can substitute **zum Anbeißen** with **zum Fressen** *[to devour]*, **zum Anknabbern** *[to nibble on]*, **zum Knutschen** *[to snog]* and **zum Dahinschmelzen** *[to melt away]* as well.

Ich hab dich zum Fressen gern.
I like you so much, I could eat you.

Sie hat 'n Narren an ihm gefressen.
She is nuts about him.
[she has devoured a fool in him]

Hitting on someone

In order to win the heart of your admired one, you'll start with **flirten** *[to flirt]*, **schäkern** *[to dally]*, **Süßholz raspeln** *[to rasp liquorice = sweettalk]*, **angraben** *[to dig on = come on to]*, **anmachen** *[to make on = turn on]*, **anbaggern** *[to excavate on = hit on]*, **umwerben** *[to woo]*, **verführen** *[to seduce]*, **aufreißen** *[to rip up = pick up]*, **bezirzen** *[to entice]*, **umgarnen** *[to enmesh]* or **sich ranmachen an** *[to make passes at someone]*. If the efforts resulted in getting the person into bed:

Ich hab sie rumgekriegt/abgeschleppt.
I won her over.
[I have gotten her around / towed her]

Du lässt auch nix anbrennen!
You don't pass up on any chance.
[you also let nothing get burned]

In the phrase nicht lange fackeln, *the word* fackeln *refers to the restless movement of an unsteadily burning flame of a torch.*
So if someone didn't flicker long, it means that they didn't 'dillydally' and wasted no time.

Der hat nich' lang gefackelt.
He didn't waste much time.

Es hat voll gefunkt.
They hit it off. *[it has fully sparked]*

Knocked back

You tried your best, but you were ultimately knocked back by the admired one: **abgeblitzt** *[struck off]*, **abserviert** *[served off]*, **'n Korb bekommen** *[got a basket]*, **abgeschossen** *[shot down]*, **geschasst** *[dumped]* or:

Ich hab mir 'ne Abfuhr geholt.
I was struck off.
[I have fetched myself a snub]

Der hat mich dumm angequatscht.
He came on to me with stupid talk.
[he has dumbly blathered me]

Before we dive into all the things the sexes say about each other, lets look at endearing terms for **Freund** [male friend]. Men also use **Kumpel** [mate] to describe a male friend or acquaintance. However, if they say **mein Kumpel** [my mate], he's a 'very good mate'.

To address a mate in a casual way, men use greetings like **Na, altes Haus?** [well, old house] which really translates into 'Hey, how are you going, my old friend?'. This is true also for **Na, alter Schwede?** [well, old Swede]. **Na, du alte Sau?** [well, you old sow] is popularly used in a tongue-in-cheek manner among blokes.

Another friendly way to address a mate in an endearing way is **Alte(r)** [old woman/-man] or **Dicke(r)** [big/fat woman/-man], no matter how old or big they are.

The term alter Schwede *was supposedly coined due to the popularity of the Swedish soldiers, who were hired as training personnel for the Prussian army by the Prussian Elector Friedrich Wilhelm I. after the 30-year-war.*

Sweetheart

When a couple sweet-talks, you'll hear endearing names like **Süße(r)** [sweetie], **Schätzchen** [little treasure], **Schatz(i),** [(little) treasure], **Schnuckiputzi, Schnuckelchen** [cutie], **Babe*** [babe], **Liebling** [darling], **Hasi** [bunny], **Mausi** [little mouse], **Zuckerschnäuzchen** [little sugar snout], **Spatz** [sparrow], **Liebste(r)** [dearest], **Täubchen** [little pigeon], **Herzblatt** [sweetheart], to name the most common.

The proper terms for girl- and boyfriend include **Freund(in)** *[boy-/girlfriend]*. If it's less serious **Geliebte(r), Lover*** *[lover]* and in Bavarian **Gspusi** *[playmate]*. Once you've past 40 years of age and prefer 'ladyfriend' over 'girlfriend', Germans tend to call the partner **Lebensabschnittsgefährte/-gefährtin** *[life section comrade (m/f)]*, which is basically saying that it's not intended for a lifetime.

Even more specific idioms for girlfriend are **Perle** *[pearl]*, **Puppe** *[doll]*, **Ische** *[missus]*, **Schnalle** *[dog's cunt]*, **Angebetete(r)** *[admired]* and **Flamme** *[flame]*. Other terms for 'boyfriend' are synonyms for 'bloke' like **Macker** and **Kerl**. If you want to describe a girl as a 'hot chick': **süße Schnecke** *[sweet snail]*, **geile Tussi** *[horny/hot chick]*, **heißes Mädel** *[hot girlie]*, **steiler Zahn** *[steep tooth]* and in the river Rhine area as **lecker Mädchen** *[tasty girl]* or **lecker Schnittchen** *[tasty slice]*.

Die Braut is' echt erste Sahne / schoko.
She's just tops.
[the chick/bride is really first cream / chocolate]

Die is' einfach rattenscharf.
She's red-hot. *[she is simply rats sharp]*

Die hat einfach das gewisse Etwas.
She's got that little something.

Die sieht verboten aus!
She looks red-hot. *[she looks prohibited]*

More idiomatic compliments include **geile Frau** [hot/horny woman], **geile Braut** [hot/horny bride], **Keule** [club], **heiße Tusse** [hot chick] and **süßes Mädchen** [sweet girl], to name a few. Men are complimented as **toller Hecht** [terrific pike], **geile Sau** [hot/horny sow] and also simply **süßer Kerl** [sweet bloke], to name a few.

Er hat einfach 'n tollen Knackarsch.
He's got such a great butt.
[he simply has a terrific crisp arse]

Er hat 'nen echt süßen Arsch.
He's got a real fine arse.
[he really has a sweet arse]

Er hat schöne Muckis.
He's got great muscles.

Der hat 'n geilen Waschbrettbauch.
He's got a hot sixpack.
[he has a hot/horny washboard belly]

Er is' 'n Bild von 'nem Mann.
He's so goodlooking.
[he is an image of a man]

Attributes for both sexes are: **süß** [sweet], **niedlich** [dinky], **knuffig, schnuffig, schnuckelig, putzig** [all: cute], **lecker** [tasty], **nett** [nice], **heiß** [hot], **cool*** [cool] and also **geil** [hot/horny].

About the Body & Intimacy

Some knowledge about intimate body-parts is essential before we get to the very climax of this book.

A woman

First there are **Brüste** *[breasts]*, **Titten** *[tits]*, **Möpse** *[boobs]*, **Memmen** *[mammory glands]*, **Hupen** *[hooters]*, **Tüten** *[bags]*, **schöne große Ohren** *[nice big ears]*, **Höcker** *[camel humps]*, **dicke Dinger** *[big things]*, **Gazongas*** *[gazongas]*, **Äpfel** *[apples]*, **Birnen** *[pears]*, **Glocken** *[bells]*, the **Busen** *[bosom]* or if not meant in a friendly way: **Euter** *[udder]*. If we go into details, you need to know **Brustwarzen** *[breast warts]* and **Nippel** *[nipples]* as well.

Die hat aber ganz schön Holz vor der Hütte!
She's got a great set of tits! *[she has indeed pretty much wood in front of the hut]*

Sie gucken mich an!
They're looking at me!

'Ne schöne Hand voll!
A nice handful.

Sie is' flach wie 'n Bügelbrett.
She's as flat as a pancake.
[she is flat like an ironing board]

Da is' nix dran.
She's got nothing. *[there is nothing on there]*

Sie hat nix unter der Bluse.
She's flat-breasted.
[she has nothing underneath the blouse]

Once the panties come off you are looking at her **Vagina** *[vagina]* or **Scheide** *[divide]*. Cutsified it's **Muschi, Mumu** or in vulgar terms it's **Möse**[1] and **Fotze**[1] *[both: cunt]*. There are many fantasy-terms like **Pflaume**[1] *[plum]*, **Lustgrotte**[1] *[lust grotto]*, **Lusthügel**[1] *[lust hill]*, **Schlitz**[1] *[slit]*, **Spalte**[1] *[crevasse]*, **Loch**[1] *[hole]*, **Bär** *[bear]*, **Ding** *[thing]*, **Feige** *[fig]*, **Dose**[1] *[box]*, **Büchse** *[can]*, **Scham** *[pubic]* and the **Pussi**[1] *[pussy]*. In more detail, you have **Kitzler** *[tickler]* or just **Klitoris** *[clit]*.

A man

Men have more words for their private parts: **Penis** *[penis]* and **Glied** *[limb]* being the proper terms, **Schwanz**[1] *[tail]* being the most popular one. The cutsifying terms are **Dödel**[1], **Lümmel,** funny ones are **Schniedel(wutz)** *[shlong]*, **Rohr**[1] *[pipe]*, **Rüssel** *[trunk]*, **Schneebesen** *[whisk]*, **Prügel**[1] *[cudgel]*, **Schwengel**[1] *[clapper]*, **Phallus** *[phallus]*, **Geschlecht** *[gender]*, **Rute** *[rod]*, **Zapfen** *[cone]*, **Zipfel** *[tip]*, **Gurke** *[cucumber/gherkin]*, **Kolben** *[cob]*, **Apparat** *[machine]*, **Ding** *[thing]* or **Teil** *[part]*. In child-talk it's **Pimmel**[1], **Pipi** or **Pillermann.**

In the erect state, you properly call it an **'ne Erektion** [*an erection*] or idiomatically **'ne Latte** [*a slat*], **'nen Ständer** [*a stand*], **'nen Harten** [*a hard one*] or **'nen Steifen** [*a stiff one*]. Someone who's got problems in this area or is accused of being a coward in general will get to hear the nasty question:

Kriegst du ihn nich' hoch?
You don't get it up?

Part of the package is a pair of **Hoden** [*testicles*], idiomatically called **Eier** [*eggs*], **Sack** [*sack*] or **Nüsse** [*nuts*]. If you are interested in further detail you probably want to know about the **Eichel** [*acorn = glans*] and **Vorhaut** [*foreskin*], which German men often leave **unbeschnitten** [*uncircumcised*].

Foreplay

One of the most vital parts of foreplay is kissing: **küssen** *[to kiss]*, **knutschen** *[to snog]*, **zungenküssen** *[to tongue kiss]*, **abküssen** *[to smother with kisses]*, **abknutschen** *[to smooch]* and **abschlecken** *[to lick off]*.

The second ingredient for intimacy is **streicheln** *[to pet]*, **liebkosen** *[to caress]*, **umarmen** *[to embrace]*, **knuddeln, knubbeln** *[both: to cuddle]*, **kuscheln** *[to snuggle]*, **schmusen** *[to smooch]*, **herzen** *[to heart]*, **drücken** *[to press]*, **kraulen** *[to fondle]*, **kneten** *[to knead]*, **abtasten** *[to feel up]* or **zärtlich sein** *[to be tender]*.

In old-fashioned terms, all of the above are referred to as **Petting** *[petting]*. More modern is **fummeln** *[to fumble = to make out]*.

Sexed up

Being charged with sexual energy is called **aufgegeilt** *[made horny]*, **angeregt** *[animated]* and with a negative connotation to it **notgeil** *[deprived horny]*. A longer phrase for men only is:

spitz/scharf wie Nachbars Lumpi
[pointy/sharp like neighbour's Lumpi (= a generic dog's name)]

To the face of the person who turns you on, you can say the following:

Du machst mich total an.
You really turn me on.

Du machst mch ganz verrückt.
You drive me crazy.

You like whatever has been suggested:

Da steh ich voll drauf!
That's just what I love.

Da drauf fahr ich total ab.
That turns me on.

The exact opposite has been introduced earlier: Das turnt* mich total ab. = That doesn't turn me on at all. Abturnen* contains really the English word 'turn' which has to be pronounced just like in English!

Das macht mich total an.
That turns me on.

Between the sheets

There's no holding back any more and the sexed-up pair will dive between the sheets: **steigen ins Bett / in die Kiste** [to climb into the bed/box], **treiben's/machen's/tun's miteinander** [to drive/make/do it with one another], **pennen miteinander** [to dorm with one another], **schieben 'ne Nummer / 'n Quickie*** [to shove a number/ quicki]. In more explicit words it's called **ficken¹** [to fuck], **bumsen¹** [to bonk], **vögeln¹** [to bird], **poppen¹** [to pop], **pimpern¹** [to shag], **knattern¹** [to shatter], **knallen¹** [to bang], **rammeln¹** [to ram], **stechen¹** [to sting], **bügeln¹** [to iron], **durchkneten¹** [to knead through] and **nageln¹** [to nail]. In order to express that this is done more than once, analogies to the animal world are popular:

rammeln wie die Karnickel[1]
[to ram like the rabbits]
bumsen wie 'n Tier[1]
[to bonk like an animal]
vögeln wie die Weltmeister[1]
[to bird like the world champions]

Der hab ich's so richtig besorgt.
I gave her a good rogering.

When men pride themselves with giving a good performance, you'll hear this phrase.

To give a blow-job is called **einen blasen**[1] *[to blow one]*, to go down on a female is called **lecken**[1] *[to lick]*. If it's all about taking it up the arse, that's generally called **arschficken**[1] *[to arse fuck]*.

If you want to talk about masturbating, you'd commonly say **masturbieren** or less often **onanieren** *[to engage in onanism]*, **sich selbst befriedigen** *[to please oneself]* and for men only: **sich einen runterholen**[1] *[to bring one down for oneself]*, **wichsen**[1] *[to wank]* or as a funny figure of speech: **fünf gegen einen spielen** *[to play five against one]*.

The goal is mostly 'to come': **kommen,** which men also call **abspritzen**[1] *[to squirt off]*. The bloke who can't do it, will be laughed at, saying:

Ihm geht keiner ab.
He can't shoot one off. *[none goes off for him]*

Sources & Further Reading

The best sources for this collection of idiomatic German were:

Apart from that, my sources were all sorts of German chat websites, TV-series and German people who have been talking in my presence during my entire life.

- **Duden Nr. 11: Redewendungen,** Bibliographisches Institut & F.A. Brockhaus AG, Mannheim 2002
- **Wörterbuch der Szenesprachen,** Dudenverlag 2000 (out of print; old link: www.szenesprachen.de/index-h.html)
- **Sag es Treffender,** Rowohlt Taschenbuch Verlag 2004
- **www.xipolis.net**
- **www.dict.cc**
- **http://wortschatz.uni-leipzig.de**

The following websites also helped remembering German idioms, where you can find much more than I could list in this book:

- www.redensarten-index.de
- http://home.arcor.de/djenzo/d_down2o.htm
- www.ruhrgebietssprache.de
- www.blueprints.de
- www.lanari.de/lexikon.htm
- www.staff.amu.edu.pl/~macbor/lexikon.htm
- http://wortgewurschtel.fantasy-boards.de
- www.bruhaha.de/jugendsprache.html
- www.behrenfamilie.de/Sprueche/lexicon.htm
- www.detlev-mahnert.de/Jugendsprache.html
- www.goethe.de/z/50/alltag/leute/phil_u.htm
- www.eltern.de/forfamily/familie_freizeit/familienleben/jugendsprache
- www.fbls.uni-hannover.de/sdls/schlobi/jugend/jug_gehrkens.pdf
- http://de.wikipedia.org/wiki/Denglisch
- http://membres.lycos.fr/tsalomon/denglish.html

This index contains almost all the words occuring in this book (for easy recognition mostly in their inflected form). At the start of the index, some important words in colloquial spelling are introduced. They do not refer to a page number, but instead show their standard German equivalent.

Nouns with (in) attached at the end show the female version for this word describing a person. Similarly, nouns with (r) at the end show the male version. Words markes with * are of English origin.

anner (= an der)
aufm (= auf dem)
aufn (= auf den)
aufs (= auf das)
ausm (= aus dem)
fürn (= für den)
is' (= ist)
isses (= ist es)
'n (= ein/einen)
'ne (= eine)
'nem (= einem)
'nen (= einen)
nich' (= nicht)
übern (= über den)

A

abchecken* 18
aberwitzig 67
Abflug 95
Abfuhr 134
Abgang 95
abgeblitzt 134
abgebrannt 114
abgebrochen 119
abgedreht 35-36

abgefahren 35-36, 63
abgefuckt* 42
abgefüllt 127
abgekanzelt 91
abgemacht 26
abgeräumt 114
abgesahnt 114
abgeschleppt 134
abgeschossen 58, 134
abgestaubt 114
abhaken 46
abklappern 120
abknutschen 141
abkönnen 45, 91
abküssen 141
ablatschen 120
abmühen 118
abplagen 118
abquälen 118
abrackern 118
Absacker 122
Abschaum 103
abschinden 118
abschlecken 141
abschminken 46

abserviert 134
absolut 19, 36
abspritzen 143
abstrampeln 118
abtasten 141
abturnen* 18
abwarten 29
abwinken 124
ach 54
achtzig 88
Acker 95
ackern 119
Adresse 34
Affäre 58
Affe 102
Affenarsch 102
affengeil 37
affenstark 37
affig 44
Ahnung 72-73
Alki 129
alle 56, 59, 65, 85, 91, 99, 115
allein 67
Allererste 37
allerletzte 40, 103

alles 26, 38, 62, 69, 92, 118
alt 42, 64, 108
Alte(r) 95, 132, 135
Amen 30
Ammenmärchen 70
amüsierten 65
anbaggern 133
anbeißen 133
anbrennen 134
andere 77, 105
anders 76
Anfall 88
Angeber(in) 81
Angebetete(r) 136
angeblafft 91
angehäuft 114
angeheitert 126
angemacht 91
angepfiffen 91
angepflaumt 91
angepisst 91
angequatscht 134
angeregt 141
angesagt 36
angesäuselt 126

angeschickert 126
angeschissen 68, 91
angeschmiert 68
angetrunken 126
angetüdelt 126
angezwitschert 126
angraben 133
Angsthase 100
anknabbern 133
anmachen 79, 91,
133
anno 43
anpampen 79
anprollen 79
Anschiss 91
anschmieren 67
anständig 124
anturnen* 18
Antwort 79
Äpfel 138
Apparat 139
Appetit 131
arbeite 119
arbeiten 118
ärger 88
arm 107
Arm/arm 68, 107,
120
Armleuchter 106
Arsch 30, 41, 47-48,
62-63, 85, 100, 102,
109, 119-120, 137
arschficken 143
Arschficker 105
Arschgeige 102
Arschgesicht 102
Arschkarte 63
Arschkeks 102
Arschkriecher(in) 108
arschlahm 44

Arschloch 102
Art 62
Asbach 43
Asche 112-114
assig 42
Ast 66, 119
astrein 27
Atem 53
ätzend 42
auch 31-32, 57, 62,
77, 116-117, 134
aufbinden 68
aufgegeilt 141
aufgerissen 119-120
aufregend 44
aufreißen 82, 133
Aufschneider(in) 81
aufsplitten* 18
Aufstand 90
aufzutragen 82
Auge 53, 57, 61, 68,
95
auschecken* 18
auseinander 54
ausgekocht 111
ausgelutscht 61
ausgerastet 89
ausgerissen 120
ausgeschlafen 129
ausgetickt 89
ausgewachsen 129
ausgewechselt 56
auspowern* 18
ausreißen 56
ausschütten 66
außer 87
ausstehen 45, 91

B

Babe* 135
Bach 62
Backen 56
baff 52
Bahnhof 71
ballern 99
Bammel 100
Banane 69
Bandit 103
bar 77
Bär 125, 139
Bären 68
Bärenhunger 131
Bart 17, 43
Bastard 105
Batzen 113
Bauch 132
Bauchlandung 126
Bauklötze 53
Bäume 56
Beautyfarm(en)* 17
bechern 122
Bedarf 32
bedient 32
bedröhnt 127
beduselt 126
befriedigen 143
begeiert 66
begossen 61
Begriff 72
begriffsstutzig 106
behämmert 44, 86
behandelt 103
beherrschen 32
Bein 65, 117, 120
beisammen 85
beißen 62, 132
bekloppt 44, 86

beknackt 44, 86
bekomme 96
bekommst 98
beleidigt 61
bematscht 59
benebelt 126
Bengel 111
beoemmeln 66
beömmeln 66
beömmelt 66
berappen 117
berauscht 126
Bereich 38
bescheuert 44, 86
beschissen 42, 59
beschränkt 44, 86,
107
beschwipst 126
Besen 57
besoffen 127
besorgt 143
Besserwisser(in) 81
Bestseller* 17
bestusst 44
Betonkopf 104
betrunken 127
Bett 142
betuppen 67
betütert 126
Beutelratte 104
bezirzen 133
Biege 95
biegen 66
Bier 48, 122
bierselig 126
Biest 108
Bild 137
billig 80, 108
Bimbam 54
Binde 122

binden 75
Binsen 61
Birne 86, 98, 129
Birnen 138
Bisamratte 104
bisschen 33, 54, 72, 128
bist 34, 86, 103
biste 34, 52, 54, 98
Blag 111
blank 84, 114
blasen 73, 96, 143
Blassen 72
Blatt 82
blau 57, 97, 127
Blaue 113
Blech 117
blechen 117
bleib 81
bleiben 48, 77
bleibt 53
blendend 55
blick 71
blicken 95
blind 57
Blockbuster* 17
blöd 44, 79, 102, 107-108
Blödian 106
Blödkopf 105
Blödmann 106
Blödsinn 69
bloß 33
blubbern 76
Bluse 139
Blüte 113
boah 51
Bock 31, 62, 111, 120
Böcke 32
Boden 93

Body* 16
Bohne 33
Bohnenstange 110
Bohnenstroh 107
bombastisch 35
Bombenstimmung 125
bongen 26
böse 128
brach 66
brat 98
brauchst 82
Brauereipferd 109
Braus 113
Braut 136-137
brechen 130
Bredouille 115
Brei 82-83, 99
breit 127
breitschlagen 27
Brett 72
Briefing* 17
bringen 33
bringt 51, 90
Bruchlandung 126
Brüderschaft 123
brüllen 65-66
Brummschädel 129
brummt 129
Brunch* 17
brunchen* 18
Brust 122
Brüste 138
Brustwarzen 138
Bubi 110
Büchse 139
Buckel 49
Bude 121, 125
büffeln 119
Bug 98

Bügelbrett 138
bügeln 142
bumsen 142-143
bunkerst 132
bunt 93
Busen 138
Butter 38

C

Casting* 16
Catering* 17
checken* 18, 71
chillen* 18
chronisch 114
Coming Out* 17
Computer* 17
Connection* 16
cool* 35, 37, 137
cooler* 19
cooles* 19
coolste* 19

D

dabei 126
Dach 98
Dachschaden 85
dachte 52
dafür 31, 39, 117
dagegen 27
dahinschmelzen 133
dahinter 81
damit 35
dämlich 106
Dampf 96
danach 32, 48
daneben 61-62, 69
danke 31-32, 87
darauf 30

darüber 88
dasselbe 43
Datei 19
Dätz 98
davon 35
davongekommen 57
dazumal 43
Deckel 98
Deez 98
demselben 42
denk 34, 52
denkste 34
denn 61, 70
dennschon 27
Depp 106
deppert 44, 86
derb 50
Desktoppublishing* 17
Desktop-publishing* 17
Dez 98
dicht 86, 127
dick 51, 54, 82, 93, 109, 138
Dicke(r) 135
Dickkopf 104
Dickschädel 104
Ding 32, 50, 54, 139
Dinger 138
dinieren 132
Dinner* 16
doch 40-44, 48-49, 51-52, 54, 68-70, 85-86, 92-93, 106-107, 125
Dödel 139
doof 44, 107
Doofkopf 105
Doofmann 106

A–Z Index

Dose 139
Döskopf 105
downgeloaded* 19
downloaden* 18-19
Drachen 111
dran 34, 98, 139
drauf 29-30, 45, 48, 120, 142
Dreck 40, 78, 103
dreckig 59, 108
Drecksack 103
Drecksau 104
Dreckschwein 104
Dreckskerl 103
Dreckspatz 111
Dreieck 90
Dreikäsehoch 110
Driss 74
dröge 44
Drückeberger(in) 101
drücken 141
drum 82
Duckmäuser(in) 101
dufte 35
dumm 44, 63, 68, 104, 107-108, 119, 134
dümmer 106
Dummheit 106
Dummkopf 105
dummschwallen 77
Dummschwätzer(in) 77
Dumpfbacke 106
Dunkeln 73
Durchblick 71
durchgebrannt 89
durchgegangen 89
durchgeknallt 44, 86
durchkneten 142

Durst 128
Dussel 106
dusslig 119

E

Ebbe 114
echt 36, 39, 41, 45, 50-51, 58, 62, 65, 70-71, 84, 87-88, 91, 101, 103, 108-109, 118-119, 125-126, 136-137
Ecken 115
egal 49
eh 27, 54
Ehrenwort 29
ehrlich 50
Ei 54
Eichel 140
Eier 84, 112, 140
eigene 63, 94
Eimer 41
einchecken* 18-19
einfach 18, 36-37, 65, 80, 83, 89, 91, 136-137
Einfaltspinsel 106
eingefangen 91
eingesackt 114
eingeschleimt 109
eingestrichen 114
einschmeißen 131
einwerfen 131
einziehen 101
Ekel 111
Elch 52
Element 56
elend 59-60, 97
Eltern 38

e-mailen* 18
Ende 65
Enden 115
englische 62
erbrechen 130
Erde 65, 117
Erektion 140
erlaubt 106
erleben 97
erledigt 26
ernst 77
erste 136
ertrag 79
erzähl 70
erzählen 75, 77
Esel 107
essen 112, 131-132
Etwas 136
Euter 138
Event* 19
ex 123
Extrawürste 118
extrem 36
ey 36-37, 50-51
Eye Catcher* 17

F

fackeln 134
Faden 68
fahr 142
fahren 30
fällig 98
fällt 51
falsch 34, 108
fängt 88
faseln 76-77
Fass/fass 51, 93
fast 51
Fatzke 103

faustdick 111
Faxen 93
fehlt 34, 115
Fehltritt 126
Feierabend 93
feige 101, 139
Feigling 101
fein 62
Fenster 64, 117
Ferkel 111
fertig 59, 78, 91, 99
fett 109, 116
fett* 36
Fettarsch 109
Fettfleck 109
Fettkloß 109
Fettsack 109
Fettsau 109
Fettwanst 109
feucht 94, 110
Feuer 57, 96
Fez 125
Fiasko 126
fick 47
ficken 142
Fiesling 111
Figur 39
Filmriss 129
find 45
findet 57
Finger 96, 119
Fisch 49, 56
Fisimatenten 70
fit 56
fix 59-60
fixe 70
flach 138
Flachwichser 104
Flamme 136
Flasche 106

Flegel 111
Fleisch 49, 63
Fliege 95
flipp 88
flirten 133
Flittchen 108
Flocken 112
Flöhe 112
Flop 126
fluppt 38
Fotze 108, 139
foxi 60
Frau 137
frei 83
freilich 30
fress 55
Fressalien 132
Fresse 54, 80-81, 97-98
fressen 132-133
freu 56
Freude 35
Freund 135
Freund(in) 136
Frosch 101
fuchsteufelswild 87
fuck* 40
Fuffi 113
fühl 55-56, 59
fummeln 141
fundum 123
für sich 39
fürn 55
fusselig 76
futtern 131
Futzi 103

G

gab 79

gaga 86
gähnend 44
Ganove 103
Gans 107
ganz 63, 68, 84, 86-87, 90, 100, 117, 128, 138, 142
Ganzes 49
gar 38, 71, 82, 94
gäu?! 36
Gauner 103
Gazongas 138
gebacken 54
Geblubber 77
gebongt 26
gebracht 125
gebruncht* 18
gecheckt* 71
Gedanken 33
gedeckt 32
gedownloaded* 19
gedreht 59
gefackelt 134
Gefährt 19
Gefasel 77
gefeiert 124
gefressen 91, 133
geführt 68
gefunkt 134
gegangen 61, 100
geh 60, 95
gehabt 57
gehauen 91, 124
geholt 57, 134
gehst 84
geht 35, 48, 55, 59, 62, 87-88, 94, 117, 125, 133, 143
Gehtnichtmehr 88
gehüpft 43

Geier 73
geiern 65
geil 35, 37, 111, 136-137
Geist 84
Geistern 86
geizig 114
gekippt 51
geklönt 74
gekniffen 63
gekriegt 57
Gelaber 73
Gelächter 66
geladen 87, 128
gelaufen 38, 61, 63
Geld 113, 117-118
Geldbeutel 114
gelegt 69
Geliebte(r) 136
geliefert 64
gell?! 36
gelletse?! 36
gemacht 26, 91-92, 125
genehmigen 122
genommen 68-69
Genörgel 79
gepeilt 71
Geplapper 77
Gequake 74
gequirlt 41
gerade 32, 34, 57, 62, 75, 114
gerädert 59
gerafft 71
gerallt 71
geringsten 33
Gerippe 110
gerissen 117
geritzt 26, 38

gern 26, 49, 115, 133
Gerücht 55
gerutscht 100
Gesabbel 77
Gesabber 73
geschafft 59
geschasst 134
geschaut 128
gescheit 86
geschenkt 26
geschickt 58
Geschlecht 139
geschmiert 38
geschnallt 71
Geschnatter 74
geschnitten 63
geschossen 62
Geschwafel 77
Geschwalle 77
Geschwätz 73
Gesicht 60
gesprungen 43
gestern 42
gestohlen 48
gestrichen 45, 100
gestrickt 42
Gesülze 73
getroffen 58
getrunken 128
gewiss 29
gewisse 136
Gewitterziege 111
Gezeter 79
gezogen 57-58, 63, 69
gibt 51, 97, 118
gicksen 67
Gift 30
Giftspritze 111
Giftzwerg 112

ging 61, 124

Glas 128

glatt 38

Glatteis 68

glaub 51

glaubst 52

gleich 88, 90, 96-99, 117

Glied 139

Global Player* 17

Glocken 138

Glück 57

göbeln 130

gold 113

Gollo 106

Gosche(n) 80

granatenvoll 128

greifen 118

Griff 62

grinsen 67

grinst 67

grölen 65

groß 29, 80-81, 117

Großkotz 81

Großmaul 81

Großmutter 77

größte 58

grottenschlecht 42

grün 38, 43, 54, 97, 117

Grundeis 100

Grünschnabel 110

Gspusi 136

gucken 28, 138

Gurke 139

Gürtel 115

gut 31, 86-87, 93

Güte 54

H

hä 70

Haar 46, 57, 70, 112

hab 19, 27, 35, 45, 57-59, 63, 66, 68, 71-72, 87-88, 91-93, 100, 114, 118-119, 121, 127, 129, 131, 133-134, 143

haben 18, 49, 68, 74, 92, 116, 124, 126

hackedicht 127

hackezu 127

Hackfleisch 99

Hahn 48

hakt 86

halb 110

Halbaffe 110

Halbes 49

halblang 80

hallo 50

Hals 45, 57, 63, 88

Halskrause 63

hälst 92

halt 55, 80-81

halten 66, 68, 88, 92

Halunke 103

Hammer 50

hammerhart 37

hammermäßig 37

Hand 29, 138

Händchen 39

Hände 96

Handy* 16

Hänfling 110

häng 65

Hänger 59

hängt 45

Hanswurst 106

Happyend* 17

Happy-end* 17

hardcore* 50

Härte 51

Harten 140

Hasi 135

hasse 45

hast 70, 72-73, 85

haste 57-58, 62, 120, 132

hat 39, 43, 53, 57-58, 81, 91-92, 100, 103, 107, 109, 111-114, 117, 125, 127-129, 133-134, 136-139

Hau 85, 95, 132

Haubitze 127

Häufchen 60

Haufen 113-114

Haus 135

Häuschen 56

Haut 33

heavy* 50

heben 122

Hecht 137

heftig 50

heilig 54

Heini 103

heiß 82-83, 92, 116, 136-137

Heißhunger 131

helfen 96, 115

hell 50

Hemd 101, 110

Henker 73, 95

heraus 58

herbeigezogen 70

herrscht 114

herunterschlingen 132

Herz 29, 100

Herzblatt 135

herzen 141

herziehen 78

Heu 113

heulen 64

heut 121

hibbelig 84

high* 19

Himmel 41, 54, 56, 73

hin 34

hinblättern 117

hingehen 49

hinhauen 28

hinstecken 47

hinten 115

hinter 110-111, 122

hinterfotzig 108

Hintern 96

hinüber 128

hip* 19, 36

hirnrissig 70

hirnverbrannt 70

Hit* 50

hoch 71, 130, 140

Höcker 138

Hoden 140

Hohlkopf 105

Hölle 92, 125

höllisch 36

Holz 138

Hölzchen 75

Holzweg 62

Honigkuchenpferd 67

Hopfen 64

hör 79, 92

hören 74

Horizont 107

Hornochse 107
hört 92
Hose 43, 61, 66, 100, 126
Hosenpisser(in) 100
Hosenpupser(in) 100
Hosenscheißer(in) 100, 110
Huhn 57, 107
Hühner 70
Hühnerkacke 40
Humbug 69
Hund 48, 51, 101, 103
Hundekacke 40
hundertachtzig 88
hundeselend 59
Hunger 131
Hupen 138
Hure 108
Hurenbock 105
Hurensohn 105
husten 96
Hut 35, 42, 46
Hütte 138
Hype* 17

I

Idee 70
Idiot 106
immer 28, 42, 71, 81-82, 125
in* 19, 36
Indianerehrenwort 29
Insider* 17
Interesse 31
intergalaktisch 35
Internet* 17
intus 127

irre 35-36, 44, 84, 86-87
Ische 136

J

ja 34, 50, 52, 56-58, 62, 70, 75, 77, 85-88, 116
Jacke 43
Jammerlappen 100
jedem 109
jenseits 128
jetzt 36, 50, 53-54, 70, 73, 76, 79-81, 92-93, 98, 101, 125-126
Job* 17
Jordan 128
juckt 48

K

kack 52
Kacke 40, 69, 74
Kaffee 42
Kahn 127
Kakao 78
kalt 42, 44, 99
Kamellen 43
Kampftrinker(in) 129
Kanacke 103
Kanaille 103
Kanal 127
Kanalratte 104
kann 28, 31-33, 35, 45, 48, 67, 74, 77, 91-92, 102, 115, 117
kannst 30, 47, 49, 77, 97, 116

kannste 30, 34, 46-47, 76-77, 82, 116
Kanone 41
Kante 122
Kapee 72, 106
Kappes 69
kaputt 59, 66, 70
Karnickel 143
Kartoffeln 57
Käse 40
Kasse 115, 117-118
Kastanien 57
Kasten 39
Kater 128-129
Katze 83
Katzenjammer 129
kau 76
kaufen 31
Kehricht 94
Keks 84
kennen 96
Kerl 136-137
Keule 137
kichern 67
Kiemen 54, 131-132
Kies 112
killen* 18
Kind 29
kippen 122
Kirche 30
kirre 84
Kirschen 112
Kiste 142
Kitzler 139
Klappe 80-81
Klappergestell 110
klappt 38
klar 26
Klärchen 26
klaro 26

Klartext 83
klasse 36
Klatsche 85
klatschen 78
Klatschtante 78
kleben 99
klein 111
Kleinholz 99
Klemme 115
klemmen 131
klinkte 89
Klitoris 139
Klo 62
klönen 74
klopfen 81
kloppen 46, 99
Klöpse 51
Kloßbrühe 26
Klugscheißer(in) 81
knabbern 132
Knackarsch 137
Knacker 112
Knall/knall 85, 99
knallen 99, 142
Knallkopf 105
Knalltüte 106
knapp 62, 115
knattern 142
knauserig 114
Kneipenbummel 121
Kneipentour 121
Knete 112, 117
kneten 141
knicken 46
knickerig 114
Knie 47
Knilch 110
Knirps 110
knöpf 96
knubbeln 141

knuddeln 141
knuffig 137
knülle 127
Knüller 50
knuspern 132
knutschen 133, 141
knutscht 52
Kohl 116
Kohldampf 131
Kohle 112-114, 117
Kokolores 69
Kolben 139
Komatrinker(in) 129
komisch 67
komm 31, 70, 83, 117
kommt 35, 45, 125, 130
komplett 53, 61
konnt 66
könnt 30, 56, 62
Könnte 28
Kopf 34, 60, 68, 70, 72, 86, 92, 129
Kopp 70
Korb 134
Korinthenkacker(in) 112
Korn 57, 68
korrekt 35
köstlich 65
Kotzbrocken 103
kotzen 44-45, 130´
kotzübel 130
krachen 124
kräht 48
krallen 131
Kram 94
krank 66
krass 50
Kratzbürste 108

kratzt 48
kraulen 141
Kreide 115
Kreuz 69
Kreuzkruzitürken 41
kreuzweise 49
kriecht 109
krieg 44, 52, 65, 88, 117
kriegen 54
kriegst 54, 140
kriegt 54
kringelig 66
kringeln 66
Krise 52
Krone 127
Krösus 118
Kröte 111
Kröten 112
krumm 66, 118
Kruzi 41
Kruzifix 41
Kruzitürken 41
kübeln 130
Kuckuck 73, 95
kugeln 66
Kuh 107-109
Kuhhaut 35
kultig 36
kümmer 94
kümmert 47
Kumpel 135
Kurve 57
Kurze(r) 110
kuscheln 141
küssen 141
küsst 52

L

labern 73
Labertasche 74
lachen 65-66, 70, 96
lahm 44
lang 61, 76, 134
langen 99
länger 82
langsam 93
Langweiler(in) 44
langweilig 44
Lappen 117
lass 31, 95, 121-123
lasse 27
lassen 27, 30
lässt 134
Lästermaul 78
lästern 78
Lästerzunge 78
Latein 65
Latschen 51
Latte 140
Latten 85
Latz 98
lau 116
laufen 61, 122
läuft 38, 131
Laus 61
Lausbube 111
lausig 42
Leben/leben 55, 113, 125
Lebensabschnittsge-fährte 136
Lebensabschnittsge-fährtin 136
Leber 61, 83
Leberwurst 61
leck 47

lecken 47, 143
lecker 18, 136-137
Leiche 60
Leichnam 60
leiden 45
Leier 42
Leine 95
leisteste 72
Leitung 72
lernen 96
Letzte 40, 103
lieb 54
Liebe 133
liebkosen 141
Liebling 135
Liebste(r) 135
Lied 42
liegen 84
liegt 39
Lippe 82
Loch 117, 139
locker 85
löffeln 131
logisch 26
logo 26
Loser(in) 101
löten 122
Lover 136
Luder 108
Luft 81, 103
Lulatsch 110
Lümmel 111, 139
Lump 103
Lumpi 141
Lusche 101
Lust 31
Lustgrotte 139
Lusthügel 139
lustig 67, 93

M

mach 50, 80, 95-96, 99, 101
machen 33, 66, 78, 82, 96, 120-121, 142
machst 53, 84, 142
macht 39, 45, 84, 91, 113, 116, 142
machte 90
mächtig 124
Macke 85
Macker 81, 136
Mädchen 136-137
Made 56
Mädel 136
Magen 133
Mailbox(en)* 17
mailen* 18
mal 28, 31-32, 47, 49, 57, 74, 76, 80-81, 83, 96, 99, 102
malochen 119
Malz 64
mampfen 131
man 77-78, 117
Mangel 99
Mann 50, 72, 81, 137
Märchen 70
markieren 81
Marsch 96
Maß 92
maßlos 88
masturbieren 143
mau 42
Maul 78, 80, 82, 97
maulen 79
Maus 93
Mäuse 112
mäusemelken 64

Mausi 135
Max 81
Meckerkuh 79
meckern 79
Meckerziege 79
Meeting* 17
mehr 51, 66, 71, 74, 79, 85, 88, 92
meins 32
Meise 85
Memme 101
Memmen 138
Mensch 50
meschugge 86
Midlifecrisis* 17
Midlife-crisis* 17
mies 104
Milchbubi 110
millionenschwer 114
miserabel 42
Missgeburt 105
Mist 40-41, 69, 74
Mistkerl 103
miteinander 142
möglich 28
Mondkalb 107
Moneten 112
Moos 112
Möpse 112, 138
Mordshunger 131
mordsmäßigen 131
Möse 139
mosern 79
Mücken 112
Muckis 137
Muffe 100
Müll 40, 69, 74, 77
mümmeln 132
Mumpitz 69
Mund 54, 76, 80, 82,

131
Münze 77
Mus 99
Muschi 139
muss 75, 77, 81-82, 94, 115
musst 82
Muster 42
Muttersöhnchen 110
Mütze 98

N

na 47, 52, 96, 110-111, 135
nä 32
Nachbar 141
nageln 142
Nähkästchen 76
Narren 68, 133
naschen 132
Nase 45, 69, 75, 93-94, 98, 113
Natter 128
natürlich 29
ne wa?! 36
ne?! 36
ned?! 36
nee 31
nehmen 30, 68, 77, 82, 99, 122
Nerv 32, 84
Nervensäge 83
nervig 83
nervst 83
nervt 19
nett 137
neugeboren 55
Neune 54
Neunmalklug 110

nid wohr?! 36
nid?! 36
nidd?! 36
nie 55, 95, 117
nieder 51
niedlich 137
Nippel 138
nix 27, 31, 35, 49, 51, 71, 81, 94, 134, 139
nö 31-32
nochmal 27, 41, 57, 80
nöd?! 36
nölen 79
Nonsens* 69
Nörgelei 79
nörgeln 79
notgeil 141
nu?! 36
nüd wahr?! 36
null 31
Nummer 142
nur 48, 63, 70-71, 116
Nüsse 140
Nutte 108

O

O.K.* 26
oberaffen- 37
oberaffengeil 37
oberaffentitten- 37
obercool* 82
oberlustig 67
Obermacker 81
Oberstübchen 86
Obertrottel 106
Ochse 107
ochsen 119

Ocken 112
od'r?! 36
öde 44
Ofen 62
offen 85
öfter 28
Ohr 45, 53, 76, 102, 110-111, 138
okay* 26
oki doki* 26
ölen 119
olle 43
onanieren 143
One-Night-Stand* 17
Opern 76
optimal 35
ordentlich 99
ordern* 18
Ordnung 26-27
outen* 18
Outfit* 16
overdressed* 19

P

paletti 26
Palme 90
pampig 79
Pappnase 106
Party* 17, 124
Patsche 115
Pauke 124
pech 63
Penis 139
pennen 142
Penner 107
Penunsen 113
Performance* 37
peripher 48
Perle 136

Pest 45
Petting 141
Pfanne 91
Pfeffer 49
pfeffern 99
Pfeife 46
pfeifen 47
Pferd 52, 77, 119
Pferde 89, 92
Pferdeäppel 67
Pflaume 139
Phallus 139
Phrasendrescher(in) 74
picheln 122
piepegal 49
Piepen 112
Pillermann 139
Pimmel 139
pimpern 142
Pimpf 110
Pipi 139
Pipifax 69
Pipikram 69
Piste 121
Plan 72
plappern 76
platt 54, 91
platzen 66
Plätzen 80
plaudern 74
Plauderstündchen 75
plaudert 76
Plaudertasche 74
plauschen 74
pleite 114, 126
plemplem 44, 86
polier 97
Polizei 106
poppen 142

Portion 110
Post 125
Prahlhans 81
Problem 33
probt 90
Prügel 97, 139
prügeln 99
prusten 66
prustete 66
Pudel 61
pumpen 115
Puppe 136
Puppen 124
pushen* 18
Pussi 139
Pute 107
Putz 124
putzig 137

Q

Quadrat 90
quaken 74
Quark 69, 74
quasseln 74
Quasselstrippe 74
Quatsch/quatsch 69, 76
quatschen 74
Quatschkopf 74
Quickie* 17, 142

R

Rabauke 111
Rad 85
rädern 59
Rage 87, 90
rammeln 142-143
randvoll 127

ranmachen 134
Rappel 88
rasend 131
Raserei 90
raspeln 133
raste 88
raten* 18
Ratte 104
rattenscharf 136
raubst 84
rauchen 46
raus 45, 82
Rausch 129
rausgelassen 124
rauswerfen 117
Recycling* 17
red 76, 82-83
Rede 35
redet 76
Regenwetter 60
Reibach 113
reiben 75
reich 114
reicht 32, 63
Reihe 54
reihern 130
rein 121, 132
Reinfall 126
reinhauen 131
reinschieben 131
reinschütten 122
reinstecken 94
reinstopfen 132
reinziehen 122
Remmidemmi 125
Rheintour 121
richtig 74, 86-87, 124, 143
riechen 91
Riesen 90, 113

Riesenarschloch 102
Riesenhunger 131
Riesenpleite 126
Riesenstunk 90
Riesenterz 90
Riesentrara 90
riesig 35
Rindvieh 107
riskieren 82
rödeln 119
Rohr 139
Rolle 121
Rotznase 110
Rübe 98
Rück 82
Ruhe 80
rum 79, 82-83
rumbrettern 120
rumeiern 120
rumgeführt 69
rumgekriegt 134
rumgondeln 120
rumgurken 120
rumkurven 120
runter 62, 84, 91
runtergeladen 19
runtergeputzt 91
runterholen 143
runterladen 19
runterrutschen 49
Rüssel 139
Rute 139

S

sabbeln 76
Sache 83
Sack 84, 140
Saftsack 103
sag 50

Sahne 37, 136
Salat 126
Satansbraten 111
satt 52
Sau 41, 91, 101, 104-105, 109, 124, 135, 137
sau- 37
sauber 52
sauer 87
Saufbold 129
saufen 123
Säufer(in) 129
Saufkumpan 121
Saufkumpel 121
Sauftour 121
saugut 37
Sauhund 104
Saukerl 104
saumäßig 37, 42
saumäßigen 131
Saus 113
saustark 37
Schabracke 111
Schacht 93
Schädel 129
Schaf 107
schaffen 119
schäkern 133
schallend 65
Scham 139
scharf 141
Schatz(i) 135
Schätzchen 135
schauen 28
schaukeln 29
Schaumschläger(in) 74
schäumt 87
scheckig 66

scheffeln 113
Scheibenkleister 40
Scheide 139
Scheiß 48
Scheiß/scheiß 47, 50, 74, 92
Scheißangst 100
Scheißdreck 40, 94
Scheiße 40-41, 58, 63, 69-70, 103
scheißegal 49
Scheißfresse 97
Scheißkerl 103
scher 95
scheuern 99
Scheunendrescher 132
Schicht 93
schicker 126
Schickse 107
schieben 47, 131, 142
schief 61, 66
schießen 66-67
Schiffbruch 126
Schifferscheiße 106
Schimmer 72
Schippe 69
Schisser(in) 100
schlackerst 53
Schlaffi 101
Schlaftablette 44
Schlag 52
Schläge 97
schlagen 27, 97, 99
Schlagseite 128
schlägt 93
Schlampe 108
Schlange 108
schlapp 66

Schlappe 126
Schlappschwanz 101
Schlauch 73
schlaucht 60
Schlaumeier(in) 81
Schlawiner 111
schlecht 33, 38-39, 78, 130
schleich 83, 95
Schleimer(in) 108
Schleimscheißer(in) 108
schlemmen 132
Schlinge 57
Schlingel 111
Schlitz 139
Schlitzohr 111
Schlückchen 122
Schluckspecht 129
Schlumpf 110
schlürfen 122
Schluss 70, 93
Schmalspurwichser 104
schmausen 132
schmieren 46
Schmierfink 111
Schmu 69
schmunzeln 67
schmusen 141
Schnabel 80
schnall 71
Schnalle 108, 136
schnallen 115
schnallst 52
Schnapsdrossel 129
schnattern 74
Schnauze 80, 93, 97
Schnecke 91, 136
Schnee 42

155

Schneebesen 139
Schneekönig 56
Schneider 58
Schnepfe 108
Schniedel 139
Schniedelwutz 139
Schnittchen 136
Schnuckelchen 135
schnuckelig 137
Schnuckiputzi 135
schnuffig 137
schnuppe 49
Schnürchen 38
schnurz 49
schnurzpiepegal 49
schoko 136
schon 27-29, 33, 43, 45, 48, 82, 127-128, 130
schön 34, 63, 68, 90, 100, 117, 128, 137-138
Schotter 113
Schrank 85
Schraube 85
Schreckschraube 111
Schrott 40, 69, 74
Schuft 103
schufte 119
Schurke 103
Schuss 62, 85
Schussel 106
Schüssel 62, 85
schwach 105, 115
Schwachkopf 105
Schwächling 100
schwafeln 76
schwallen 76
Schwanz 101, 139
Schwanzgesicht 105

Schwanzlutscher 105
schwarz 34, 88
Schwarze 58
schwatzen 73
Schwätzer(in) 74
Schwede 135
Schwein 57, 104, 109
Schweinebacke 104
Schweinehund 104
Schweinepriester 104
Schwengel 139
schwer 72, 106
schwimmen 113
Schwips 127
schwöre 29
Schwuchtel 105
schwul 105
Schwung 125
Sciencefiction* 17
Science-fiction* 17
Sechseck 90
Seilrolle 121
selber 52, 67
selbstverständlich 29
Sender 84
Senkel 84
Sense 93
Sesselpuper(in) 44
setzt 97
setzte 89
shit* 17, 40
sicher 30
Sicherung 89
siehst 60-61, 64, 67
sieht 133, 136
simsen* 18
Sintflut 48
sitzen 127
sitzt 63
SMSen* 18

so 27, 30, 32, 41, 43-44, 74, 79, 82, 88, 117, 124, 143
Song* 17
sonst 87
sonstwohin 47
sowas 50
spaced* 19
spachteln 132
Spalte 139
Spanner 111
Spargeltarzan 110
Spaßverderber(in) 101
Spatz 135
Spatzenhirn 107
Specht 39
Speck 56
Speichellecker(in) 108
speien 130
speisen 132
speiübel 130
Sperenzkes 70
spielen 61, 143
Spielverderber 101
Spielverderber(in) 101
Spießer(in) 112
Spinatwachtel 111
spinne 51
spinnen 51, 86
Spinner 106
spinnst 86
spitz 141
Spitzbube 111
spitze 35-36, 55
spitzenmäßig 37
Spökes 70
Sprache 53, 82
spricht 27

springt 90
Sprüche 81
Sprung 85
Sprünge 96
spuck 83
Spucke 53
spucken 130
Spur 65
Stadt 121
Ständer 140
ständig 78-79
Stange 113
stänkern 79
stark 35, 37, 51
stärken 131
Staub 95
staunst 53
stechen 142
stecken 31, 46-47, 75
steh 45, 52, 61, 115, 142
steht 60, 63, 92
Steifen 140
steigen 142
steil 136
Stein 116
steinreich 114
stellst 34
stempeln 119
sternhagelvoll 128
stimmt 55
stinksauer 87
Stinkstiefel 112
Stinktier 112
Stinkwut 87
Stock 128
stockbesoffen 128
stockbetrunken 128
Stöckchen 75
stocksauer 87

stoned* 19
Story* 17, 43
strahlst 56
stramm 127
Strandhaubitze 127
streicheln 141
Strich 68
stritzebesoffen 128
Strohsack 54
Strolch 111
strunzen 73
Stück 51, 103
Sturkopf 104
sturmfreie 121
Sturz 128
sturzbesoffen 128
sturzbetrunken 128
Stuss 69
süffeln 122
sülzen 73
Sumpfhuhn 107
supergeil 36
supermäßig 37
Suppenhuhn 107
süß 136-137
Süße(r) 135
Süßholz 133

Tacheles 83
tafeln 132
Tag 60, 76
tangiert 48
Tante 78, 108
Tasche 118
Tasse 106
Tassen 85
Täubchen 135
Team* 17

Tee 29, 127
Teil 27, 41, 46-47, 139
Teppich 81
Terz 90
Teufel 73, 95
Thema 26
tickste 87
Tief 59, 118, 128
Tier 143
tierisch 88
Tinte 26, 63, 115
Tisch 69, 123
Titten 138
tja 27
Tobak 43
Tod 45
Tode 88, 119
toll 137
Tollpatsch 106
Tölpel 106
Tonne 46, 109
Top Tens* 17
toppen* 18
Toptens* 17
tot 66, 126
total 36, 65-66, 83, 86-87, 89, 91, 114, 128, 142
totlachen 66
Tour 70
Tracht 97
Trampel 106
Transe 105
tratschen 78
Tratschtüte 78
treiben 142
trendy* 19
treten 46
tricksen* 18

tricky* 19
trifft 52
trinken 29, 122-123
Trinker(in) 129
tritt 52
Trollo 106
Tropf 107
Tropfen 116
Trost 86
Tröte 107
trüb 106
Trulla 107
Trunkenbold 129
Tucke 105, 111
tun 142
Tunte 105
Türken 41
Turnschuh 56
turnt* 18
Tusnelda 107
Tusse 137
Tussi 37, 107, 136
tuten 73
Tüten 138
Type 91, 103

U 68
übel 38, 130
überall 94
überfragt 72
übergeben 130
überleg 28
Ufer 105
ultracool 36
umarmen 141
umgarnen 133
umwerben 133
umwerfend 35-36

unanständig 114
unbeschnitten 140
uncool* 19
underdressed* 19
unerträglich 79
ungut 31
unsicher 121
unterbelichtet 107
updaten* 18
uralt 43
urkomisch 67

Vagina 139
verachten 38
veräppeln 67
verarschen 67
verarscht 68
verboten 136
verbraten 118
verbrezelt 42
verbuttert 118
verdammt 36, 40-41, 80, 102, 106
verdient 113
verdreschen 99
verdrücken 131
verdufte 95
verflixt 41
verflucht 40-41, 102
verführen 133
vergackeiern 67
Vergasung 124
vergehen 96
vergeigt 42
vergessen 46
vergeudet 118
vergiss 108
vergrätzt 87

T

U

V

verhauen 42
verhökern 116
verjubelt 118
verkauft 68
verkehrt 38
verklickern 75
verkohlen 67
verkorkst 42
verlassen 30, 86
Verlierer(in) 101
verlinken* 18
verloren 64
vermasselt 42
vermöbeln 99
vermögend 114
vermurkst 42
verpassen 99
verpatzt 42
verpfuscht 42
verpiss 95
verprasst 118
verpulvert 118
verputzen 131
verrückt 44, 84, 86, 142
versaut 42
verschachern 116
verschärft 35
verscheißern 67
verscherbeln 116
verschlagen 53
verschleudern 116
verschlingen 132
verschwendet 118
verschwinde 95
versohlen 99
verspeisen 131
verspielt 118
versprochen 29
versteh 71

verticken 75, 116
vertilgen 131
verwetten 30
verwettet 118
verzählen 75
verzieh 95
verzockt 118
Vieh 103
viel 76-77, 88
vielleicht 28, 59
Visage 97
Vogel 58, 85
vögeln 142-143
voll 36-37, 39, 41, 44-45, 58, 61, 63, 69, 74, 83, 92-93, 100, 113, 122, 125-128, 134, 138, 142
vollfressen 132
vollgetankt 127
vollkommen 56, 84
vollschlagen 132
volltexten 76
Volltrottel 106
volltrunken 127
vorbei 48, 62
Vorhaut 140
vormachen 68
vorne 115

W

wa?! 36
Waffel 85
Wahnsinn 50
wahnsinnig 36, 87
Wahnsinnshunger 131
wahr 51
Wald 52
Walz 121

wandelnd 60
war 37, 62, 88, 125-126
wär 34, 51, 122
waren 65
warte 111
warten 34
was 39-41, 47-48, 52-54, 70, 75, 82, 96-97, 102-103, 107, 115, 125, 131-132
Waschbrettbauch 137
Waschlappen 101
Wasser 56, 63, 131
Wasserfall 76
Wecker 84
weder 49
weg 53, 64, 83, 85
weghauen 122
wegschmeißen 66
wegzischen 122
wehtäte 106
Weibstück 108
weich 99
Weichei 100
weinselig 126
weiß 28, 60, 73
Weißglut 90
weißt 47
welche 61
Wellenlänge 39
Wellness Center* 17
Weltmeister 143
wen 48, 76
wennschon 27
werd 51, 96-97, 99, 122-123
wichsen 143
Wichser 104
Wicht 110

Wichtigtuer(in) 81
Widerling 111
wieder 63, 74, 76, 95, 109
wiehern 65
will 72
Willi 107
willst 68
willste 61
windelweich 99
windsurfen* 18
Winzling 110
wird 26, 33, 93, 96
wirklich 51, 93
wirst 96
wischen 99
witzig 67
wohl 50, 53, 62, 68, 72-73, 85-86, 127-128
wohlhabend 114
Wolf 59
Wolkenbruch 41
woll?! 36
worauf 30
Workflow* 17
Wucht 36
wund 119
Wunder 97
würd 115
Wurs(ch)t 49
Wut 87

X

X 68
Xanthippe 111

Y

Yuppie* 17

Z

Zahn 136
Zähnen 112
Zahnfleisch 60
Zapfen 139
zärtlich 141
Zaster 113

Zaun 85
zechen 122
Zecher 129
Zechtour 121
Zeiger 84
zerreißt 78
zetern 79
zick 79
Zicke 107
Ziege 107, 109
zieh 95, 98
ziehen 78, 118, 122
ziehst 60

Zimtzicke 108
Zipfel 139
zischen 122
zu 127
Zuckerschnäuzchen 135
Zug 63
zugedröhnt 128
zugelötet 128
zugenäht 41
Zuhälter 105
zumute 32
zungenküssen 141

zurückhalten 32
zusammen 77, 131
zusammengeschissen 91
zusammenkratzen 117
zusammenstauchen 99
zutexten 76
Zweig 117
Zwerg 110
Zwirn 41
zwischen 131-132
zwitschern 122

The Author

Elfi H. M. Gilissen was born in Germany in 1969. Her mother is Flemish and her Dutch father is from Limburg in the Netherlands. After living in the Netherlands as a small child until 1976, her parents returned to Germany. It was there that she undertook her education, culminating in a degree at the University of Bonn in the field of translation (Chinese and Indonesian).

After working for some years in Bonn, Cologne and Bielefeld, she moved to her 'home country', the Netherlands, to live with her Australian partner. Since then, she has written a number of books for Reise Know-How on various Australian topics, such as culture shock in Australia as a visitor, experiencing the outback and bush, a Sydney travel guide, the uniqueness of Australian English and a guide on how to immigrate to Australia. In the Kauderwelsch series, she has written further books on American English, Flemish and Dutch Slang.

Having written the latter on Dutch Slang, it was then that she had the idea to write a similar book focussed on German slang, but this time written in English. Elfi continues to publish, with more titles already in the planning.